*Mending and Restoring
Upholstery and Soft Furnishings*

Mending and Restoring Upholstery and Soft Furnishings

WILL MORTON AND
NELLIE RICHARDSON

GARNSTONE PRESS

MENDING AND RESTORING
UPHOLSTERY AND SOFT FURNISHINGS
is published by
Garnstone Press Limited
59 Brompton Road, London SW3 IDS

© Will Morton and Nellie Richardson, 1973
© Illustrations: Garnstone Press, 1973

ISBN: 0 85511 390 1

Photographs by Brian Boothby
Line drawings by the authors

Filmset and printed by
BAS Printers Limited, Wallop, Hampshire

Contents

Introduction

When soft furnishings wear out, or when a move to a new home means that the curtains no longer fit the windows, there is probably no need to throw them away and buy expensive new materials. And when a favourite sofa sags in the middle, or an easy chair picked up at a jumble sale needs re-upholstering, it may not be necessary to call in expensive professional help. With patience and common sense most simple repairs can be carried out successfully by the interested amateur. We have both discovered, through teaching in adult evening classes, that a great many men and women really enjoy working with their hands and are happy to expend the necessary time and trouble.

It is, of course, a little difficult to explain craft handi-work on paper. Ideally student, teacher, and the work in hand should all be present and techniques demonstrated. But our aim here has been to condense simple, explicit instructions into the book and to supply plenty of diagrams and photographs, thereby making each step abundantly clear.

We both hope that this book will open up new possibilities of home improvements for you, that it will save you unnecessary expense and, most of all, that you will enjoy using it.

W.M.

N.R.

PART ONE

Mending and Restoring Upholstery

CHAPTER ONE

Assessing the Problems

It is almost certainly unnecessary to warn you not to attempt a repair on a very rare or valuable piece of furniture. An upholsterer is a craftsman who has served a long apprenticeship and no book can pass on his skills to that extent. However, if your favourite easy chair is sagging there is no reason why, with care and patience, you should not effect a very satisfactory repair; and there are numerous other repairs, outlined in the following pages, which are well within the capabilities of the practically minded amateur.

Old pieces of upholstered furniture can be picked up in sale rooms and junk shops for next to nothing and it might be no bad idea to rescue some cheap, tired old chair and practice on it. You will soon find out how much natural skill you have, and how much patience. Patience is vital. If you try to hurry you will almost certainly spoil the job.

Once you have decided that a particular repair job is within your capabilities, you must then gauge just what is required. A straightforward re-cover job on an armchair is fairly simple, especially if, as you remove the old cover, you observe carefully how it was originally placed. If you have to work on the springs and stuffing the job will be somewhat less simple.

Choice of covering material needs very careful consideration. Some attractive coverings are too thin – upholstery material must be strong enough to stand firm handling and plenty of wear. If you choose a patterned material you do not only have to decide whether or not the pattern is suitable for the article in question but also whether or not you are giving yourself unnecessary problems, because you will have to match up the pattern at every join.

If chair or sofa arms or backs look 'hollow' it may be that a little extra stuffing is all that is needed. But you would be well-advised to investigate to ensure that the springs and hessian below are in good order. You may find that new webbing on a sagging seat will be sufficient and that you can thus avoid the labour of a complete new seat.

You may well decide to attempt restoration on a piece of period furniture which has what is termed 'show wood'. This term applies to exposed edges of wood around the base of the chair or around the back and even on parts of the arms. This show wood will be polished, painted or even gilded and great care must be exercised to avoid damage by stray knocks with a hammer, scratches with a needle point, and so on. To minimise these risks, a curved needle instead of a straight one is recommended and a cabriole or narrow-headed hammer (see next chapter). I would also recommend that you hold a strip of cardboard against a polished edge or moulding when using a hammer; and that if you need to use a webbing stretcher against a finished surface you put a pad of velvet or soft, woolly material under the stretcher. These precautions call for a little extra time and trouble but are well worth it.

The instructions in the following pages should see you through all the common, general repair jobs likely to come your way – but when it comes to choice of materials and assessment of final results you must fall back, every time, on your own judgement.

W.M.

CHAPTER TWO

Tools and Materials

The tools and materials required will depend a great deal on the job in hand, but those tools listed below really form a basic kit. Most of them are available in Ironmonger's Shops or Do-it-Yourself Stores. Sometimes a small local repair business may oblige with odd bits and pieces. A mail order firm whose address might prove useful is: Russell Trading Co. Ltd, 75 Paradise Street, Liverpool LI 3BP. All prices given were correct at the time of going to press but may have risen since.

In an upholsterer's workshop, most work is done on a pair of trestles, but these are probably not readily available in the home. Much of the work can be done on a kitchen table or carpenters' bench – and this is preferable to working at floor level. One thing that must be borne in mind is that when doing this work there is bound to be a fair amount of dust and waste, and tacks may fly, so if at all possible the garage or garden shed is the ideal place to work.

TOOLS

Hammers

LIGHTWEIGHT (£1.50). Obviously suitable for tacking. Usually has a claw at the back end for removing temporary tacks.

MAGNETIC (£1.40) is available but is not advised for beginners.

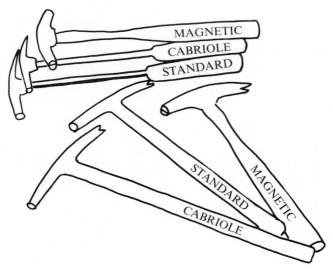

FIG. 1. A selection of hammers.

CABRIOLE (£1.70). A much lighter type, specifically for use on furniture with polished frame edges.

Knife

(20p) A straight bladed tool – very useful during cutting stages and for trimming edges.

Needles

STRAIGHT NEEDLES (6p) are of two types – bayonet point and smooth point. Obtainable in lengths from 6 to 14 inches and with slight variations in thickness (gauge).

SPRING NEEDLE (20p). Partially bent, of heavy gauge, primarily to sew in springs but has other uses as well.

CIRCULAR (5p). A needle of semi-circular shape ranging from one inch in diameter to 4 inches.

Rasp

(70p). A coarse file to take off sharp edges and to champher a frame where necessary.

Regulator

(25p). A tool pointed at one end and flattened at the other. Mostly used during stitching processes but quite useful at other times.

Ripping Chisel

(60p). A tool similar to a screwdriver, used in conjunction with a mallet to remove tacks when ripping down upholstered work.

Scissors

(85p). Upholsterers' scissors are about 9 inches overall. A heavier scissor than dressmakers' because the materials to be cut are of a coarser nature.

Skewers

(10p). 3 or 4 inches in length. Used for pinning materials in place and essential for certain forms of upholstered work.

NEEDLES

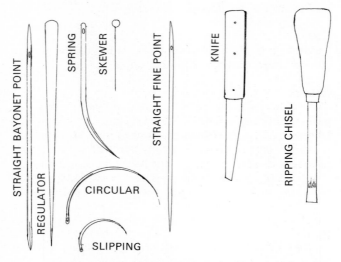

FIG. 2. Needles, knife and ripping chisel.

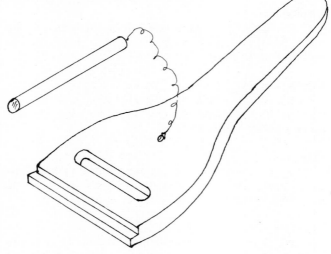

FIG. 3. Webbing stretcher.

Tape Measure
(18p). Usually a linen tape of 5 feet in length. Essential to measure rounded, shaped surfaces.

Webbing Stretchers
(55p). For straining the webbing – the most popular type is illustrated in Fig. 3.

Yardstick or Metrestick
(85p). Useful for marking out and as a straight edge.

MATERIALS

Brass Nails
In antique or brass finish, sold in boxes of 1000 at 85p per box. D.I.Y. stores may have packets of smaller quantities at proportionate prices. (Cheaper nails are made of steel and brassed over.)

Calico
Plain cotton weave material of a wide range of widths and qualities. Generally used in 36, 50 and 72 inch widths. The unbleached grade is mostly used in the trade. Prices vary from 20p to 85p per yard.

Copydex
A synthetic adhesive supplied in tubes at 9p each. A number of proprietary products are suitable.

Fibre
Of two types – Coir (coconut) and Algerian, priced at about 10p per pound. Probably difficult to obtain in small quantities.

Hair
Today generally supplied as a mixture of horse hair and cow hair in several grades at an average price of 40p per pound. An expensive filling, and also difficult to obtain in small quantities.

17

FIG. 4. Tacks, staples, gimp pins and brass nails.

Heavy Gauge Wire
   A suitable thickness is No. 8, sold at 6p per foot.

Hessian
   Woven of jute in various widths. There is a range of qualities – 10 ounce being about average. Prices vary from 27p to 65p per yard.

Hide
   Cowhide specified for upholstery is sold by the square foot at prices ranging from 60p to 90p in a large range of colours. Generally supplied as a full skin, though pieces cut to size are obtainable at higher cost.

Imitation Leather
   Woven cloth base with surface sprayed on. From 50 to 51 inches wide. Supplied in a range of qualities at £1.00 to £1.80 per yard.

Plastic Wood
   Paste-like substance supplied in tubes at 7p each.

PVC
   See Imitation Leather.

Scotch Glue
   Of animal origin. Made from hoof, offal and bones.

Sold today in bead or crystal form, though obtainable in slab by the pound. To prepare for use, boil in water.

Scrim

Similar to hessian but woven of flax and therefore of lighter weight. From 28p to 60p per yard.

Springs

DOUBLE CONE SPRINGS are the type used in traditional upholstery. These are made from steel spring wire of different thicknesses ranging from 8 to 14, and of heights ranging from 3 inches to 12 inches. The thicker gauges – 8, 9 and 10 – are used for seats and the 11, 12, 13 and 14 are for arms and backs.

SINGLE CONE SPRINGS are used only in spring units.

TENSION SPRING (Stretch spring and cable spring are other names). A suspension of a different form, hooked to the frame and strained across at tension.

Tacks

In quantity 7 pound bags are recommended, but otherwise obtainable in 1 pound, $\frac{1}{2}$ or $\frac{1}{4}$ pound packets. Prices vary with size of tack, but average 20p per pound.

Upholsterers' Cane

A flexible cane usually supplied in $\frac{3}{8}$ inch diameter and lengths of about 12 to 14 feet. Sold by weight at 10p per pound.

Wadding

A cotton-wool like material made up in 1 pound bundles at 25p to 50p per pound.

Webbing

Woven of jute, mostly 2 inches wide and obtainable at $2\frac{1}{2}$ inches width. In natural fawn colour or black and white (grey). Average price 5p per yard.

19

CHAPTER THREE

Glossary of Terms and Procedures

Braid
Woven edge trimming of cotton, wool, rayon and silk. Usually about $\frac{1}{2}$ an inch in width; with various designs.

Bridle Ties
Loops of twine distributed over hessian to hold fibre or hair stuffing in place.

Buckram
Jute woven hessian, impregnated and stiffened with glue.

Champher
The shaped-off edge of a wooden rail.

Clout Nails
Supplied in $\frac{1}{2}$, $\frac{5}{8}$ and $\frac{3}{4}$ inch lengths.

Cushion Seat
See photograph on page 43.

Ditch
See Gutter.

Flys
See Stretcher.

Fringe
Trimming decoration, usually around base of chair.

Full Seat
See photograph on page 34.

Gimp
Similar to Braid.

Gimp Pins
Small-headed tacks of $\frac{3}{8}$, $\frac{1}{2}$ and $\frac{5}{8}$ inch sizes, usually coated with an enamel or galvanised. Use for fixing braid and gimp or the exposed edges of a cover.

Gutter
Division behind front row of springs on spring edge. See illustration on page 46.

Hand slipped
The hand sewing of cover material. eg; the joining of outside backs and outside arms, or border and seat.

Laid Cord
A string made from hemp, used for tying down springs.

Mitred
A join made at a 45 degree angle, see page 81.

Repeat
In woven fabrics, this is the length measure of the design, 'repeated' through the length of the cloth.

Ruche
A trimming used on cushion edges and facings.

Scrim
Similar to hessian and used over stuffing when making traditional stitching.

Show Wood
Exposed part of framework, usually polished, gilded or painted.

Slip Knot
A form of knot on twine or cord which allows a loop to tighten up when pulled.

Spring edge work
Upholstered seating with springs placed on front edge rails.

Stretchers
Strips or pieces of hessian sewn on seat arms and back cover to pull through and tack down.

Stuffing Ties
Twine ties pierced through stuffing. See photograph on page 39.

Template
Pattern of a shape, generally cut from thin card.

Tuft
A twine tie put through a section of stuffing, as in a mattress.

Webbing
A woven strip of an average width of 2 to $2\frac{1}{2}$ inches, made from jute, jute and cotton, or jute and flax.

Webbing Stretcher
See illustration on page 16.

Whipped
A method of binding cane on to springs, generally using twine.

CHAPTER FOUR

Estimating and Cutting Material

Measuring the amount of material needed to cover a stool top or a panel-backed chair is not difficult, but easy chairs and sofas are not quite so straightforward and a certain amount of calculation is necessary to arrive at the correct quantity.

If you are doing a simple re-covering job, the old material, carefully removed, will give you something to go on. But if you are doing more detailed work on the chair – re-stuffing, putting in new springs and so on – then you must not take measurements until the work is at its final 'calico' stage and you are ready to put on the new cover.

Outside pieces are fairly easy to measure, remembering that you should allow 2 inches for turning in and tacking. Inside pieces are a little more difficult; make sure that your measurements exceed the visible area. It is usual to allow between 3 and 4 inches on each section beyond the point where the seat meets the arms and the back.

Measurements are taken, and generally tabulated (as applicable) so:

Seat	(S)	32″ × 25″
Inside Arm	(IA)	24″ × 30″
Inside Back	(IB)	33″ × 28″
Outside Arm	(OA)	18″ × 29″

Outside Back	(OB)	28″ × 24″
Border	(Bor)	11″ × 25″
Cushion	(C)	22″ × 20″
Cushion Border	(C. Bor)	5″ × 22″
Facings	(Fac)	18″ × 6″
Back Border	(BB)	$5\frac{1}{2}$″ × 25″
Inside Wing	(IW)	20″ × 12″
Outside Wing	(OW)	19″ × 10″

The first column of figures are measured on the length run of the fabric. Precise shaping is best done after the pieces have been cut (unless a template has been prepared) or as work proceeds and waste is cut away.

In order to avoid waste you will have to use common sense and plan the cutting out carefully. The best plan is to cut yourself a paper pattern for each piece required and lay them out on the material as compactly as possible. You can then outline the shape of each piece, on the wrong side of the fabric, with tailor's chalk – and be sure that you don't miss any out!

Plain materials are straightforward enough, but if you are working with patterned material you will have to give consideration to the placing of the design, particularly where sections join. If you are re-covering a sofa you will find that the areas are so large that you will have to join widths of material on seat, inside back, outside back and borders. Again, a patterned material presents its own problems at these points.

If you are working with a pile fabric, such as velvet, remember that the pile should always brush forwards on the seat and downwards elsewhere.

When you are estimating the quantities needed to cover furniture with woven fabrics, the result arrived at is in linear yards, but when you are working with leather or hide of any kind the answer is in square feet. (The term 'leather' refers not only to cowhide but also to goatskin and sheepskin; when dealing with these last two you will find that the wastage rate can be quite high because they are relatively small in area).

The best procedure is to cut a template for each piece

required – using calico for the shaped (rounded) pieces. An average cowhide is 50 square feet, and as there is no defined pattern the templates can be set at any angle and you can plan on a jig-saw principle and make your cuts to the best advantage.

Generally, the best part of the hide is in the centre – the backbone. The outside edges are stretchy and occasionally there may be a scar or a blemish. Plan your cuts to use the better hide for the inside pieces. Because of the irregular shape of a skin, an additional allowance must be made for waste – even as much as $33\frac{1}{3}\%$. These days hide costs probably about £30 a skin or 75p a square foot, so mistakes will be expensive.

CHAPTER FIVE

The Stool or Drop-in Seat

Re-upholstering a rectangular stool seat, or a rectangular drop-in chair seat, is a relatively simple piece of work.

First you will have to remove the old cover and upholstery materials. To do this you should use a ripping chisel and mallet, and be careful to work in line with the grain of the timber frame. A pair of pliers will come in useful to remove obstinate tacks. Usually you will find that the sequence of breakdown will go as follows; first the top cover, with possibly a calico cover beneath; next you will have to cut twines to release the stuffing and finally you will come to a piece of hessian and the basic webbing. Work carefully and note the sequence of layers. You will gain an understanding of the make-up of the seat which will be helpful to you when you begin to re-upholster.

The first step is new webbing. The old webbing may have given you an idea of spacing, but the general rule is to leave a space of approximately the width of a piece of webbing between each. For fixing webbing one generally uses $\frac{5}{8}$ inch improved tacks, but if the frame of the stool is of a light construction it would be wiser to use $\frac{1}{2}$ inch improved tacks, to reduce the risk of splitting the wood.

Take an end of the roll of webbing, fold over about an inch, and attach it to the frame rail with five tacks in a staggered formation in the centre of the wood. Stretch the webbing across the frame with the webbing stretcher (see Fig. 9) and attach it to the opposite frame rail with three tacks. The tension should be taut but not excessive. Cut the webbing, leaving sufficient to fold back and secure with two tacks. Repeat this operation until the required number of webs are in position. Next, fix the webbing the other way across the frame, in exactly the same manner, but this time weaving it in and out of the first row of webs.

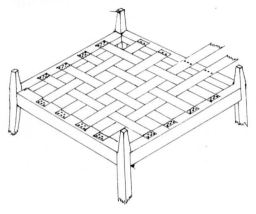

FIG. 5. Webbing of the seat.

Over the webbing stretch a piece of 10 ounce hessian, which should be one inch larger all round than the stool frame. Strain it tight and tack it with $\frac{3}{8}$ inch improved tacks over the webbing; then fold the extra back and put in another line of tacks.

If you wish to use the old hair stuffing again it will be necessary to 'tease' it, pulling it about and loosening it as much as possible. But if this old material has been in place for a very long time you will probably make a neater job with new hair stuffing.

Insert loops of twine. These are called bridle ties and are put in with a spring needle (see Fig. 6). The twine should be threaded through at about 6 inch intervals,

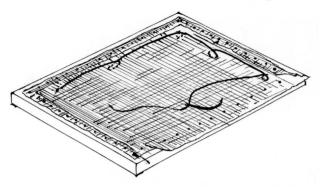

FIG. 6. Stool top; showing the tacking of the hessian and bridle ties.

looped in a continuous line. The hair should be placed under these loops, picked over and spread to cover the area and to form a mass of even density.

You must use judgement to achieve an equal quantity all over, fully an inch deep.

Over the hair stretch a piece of calico, putting in temporary $\frac{3}{8}$ inch tacks underneath the frame.

Now, starting from the centre of the frame, release one tack, pull the calico tight, and put in a permanent $\frac{3}{8}$ inch tack under the frame. Work along from this point, forming the shape of the seat as you go. Adjust the stuffing as you work to form a smooth slope to the frame edge. Do not bring any stuffing over the side of the frame. The tacks should be placed about $1\frac{1}{2}$ to 2 inches apart along the four sides of the seat. At the corners you will need to cut away surplus material to make a neat finish.

Lay wadding evenly over the seat. The final cover should be tacked, pulled tight, and finished in exactly the same manner as the calico cover, ensuring that any pattern is correctly centred.

Finally, the underside of the seat should be covered with a piece of hessian or black linen; neatly finished with a turned in edge and fixed with tacks, leaving a narrow margin all round.

FIG. 7. Final cover with corner cut away to form pleat.

An alternative method is to use a foam filling. Web and canvas the frame as described above and then, instead of hair, use polyester foam. This is supplied in sheet form and a piece cut full size and of 1 to $1\frac{1}{2}$ inches thick will be suitable. Foam is of varying hardness, or density, and you will have to use your initiative when making your selection – but bear in mind that you need a fairly high density for a seat. If the piece you use is a remnant, and has to be trimmed to size, use a pair of scissors with serrated blades or a keen-edged knife.

Apply an adhesive (Evostick or Bostic are suitable) along the frame edge, on webbing and hessian, and to the underside of the foam. Place the foam in position and press down firmly. The covering material can now be set directly onto the foam, without the intervening wadding, tacked off underneath and a bottom hessian fixed as described above.

CHAPTER SIX

The Easy Chair

All kinds of things can go wrong with an easy chair and all kinds of steps can be taken to put them right. Most of the restoration work described below is also applicable to settees and sofas.

Putting a new seat in an easy chair is one of the most frequently attempted tasks.

First of all, turn the chair upside-down and, using the ripping chisel and mallet, remove the bottom canvas. You will see that the seat cover is tacked on to the front rail, the outside arm covers onto the side rails and the outside back cover onto the back rail. Remove all these tacks to release the cover, but work carefully to avoid damage to the material which will be set back in place later. Release the material covering the arms and back for about 10 inches above the bottom rails. This may be tacked down with gimp pins or brass nails or stitched. Underneath the cover you may find wadding, which will need to be folded back, and also hessian, which again must be released and folded back.

Stand the chair on its feet and pin back the freed materials. Now you will be able to see quite a lot of tacking on the top of the base rail. All of this will have to be released. The various layers will come away in order. Generally, the arms and back covering are tacked along here, over the seat cover, but there can be slight differences in construction. Take notes as you proceed because everything will have to be replaced later. When you have removed the seat cover place it carefully to one

FIG. 8. Easy chair showing 'full' seat.

side because this, too, will be replaced later.

Once all this ripping is done the webbing can be released and the seat will drop through in a dusty mass. Now, principally with the use of a sharp knife, the twines, stitched rolls, spring ties and lashings can be cut away and the whole separated.

Decisions will now have to be made about the materials. Springs can be put back providing they are in a reasonable condition, but crippled or bent springs must be replaced with new ones. Decisions about springs really require some experience, so if in doubt you will be well advised to get new ones. The old stuffing – if it is hair or fibre – can be picked over, loosened (a rather dusty and tedious job) and put back, although it will probably be necessary to add a little extra. Other materials – webbing, hessian, scrim, etc., can be disposed of.

Before you rebuild the seat it is advisable to examine the frame and to be satisfied that the joints are sound and none of the rails split. Certainly it is pointless to upholster a damaged frame as it could break further soon after completion. A loose joint could well be successfully strengthened with some glue run into it. More extensive damage may require expert help.

Turn the chair upside-down once more, on the floor or on trestles, according to what equipment you have.

Fix the webbing, allowing a space about the width of a web between each. Start at the front rail. Fold over an inch of the end of the webbing and tack it down with five $\frac{5}{8}$ inch tacks in a staggered formation. Stretch the webbing to the back rail, using the webbing stretcher

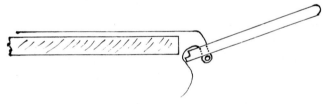

Fig. 9. Using webbing stretcher.

(see above), making sure it is taut, and knock in three $\frac{5}{8}$ inch tacks. Cut the webbing, allowing enough to fold over the end and drive in two more tacks. When you have fixed the required number of webs from front to back, fix the webbing across the frame from side to side in the same manner, commencing at the front of the frame and weaving the webbing in and out of the existing strips, (see Fig. 10.)

Turn the chair upright once more so that it is ready

to receive the springs. Usually there are 9 springs in an easy chair seat, although sometimes there are 12. You will know how many to put in by how many you removed in the first place. They should be evenly distributed over the area in straight lines – neither set too close to the rails nor bunched in the centre. Thread a spring needle with a length of twine. Stab the needle up through the webbing from underneath, alongside the coil of the first spring. Pass the twine over the spring coil and stab the needle back through to the underneath where you should make a firm knot. Repeat this operation at four equidistant points on the spring. In this manner secure each spring in its place.

The next job is to lash the springs. The purpose is to tie the springs together and so keep them in an upright position. In the process they will be pulled down, perhaps an inch or an inch and a half. Use a strong, laid cord and make two knots to each spring. (See Fig. 11.)

Strain a piece of good, strong, 12 ounce hessian over the springs. Tack it down with $\frac{1}{2}$ inch tacks, turn over

FIG. 10. Springs sewn to webbing.

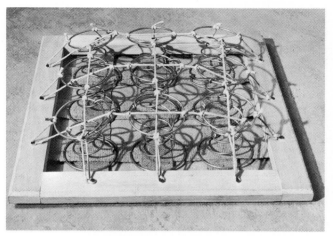

FIG. 11. Springs lashed into position.

the edge and tack down with a second row of tacks. Now sew the springs to the hessian in the same way as you sewed them to the webbing – an easier procedure at this stage because you are working from the top. (See Fig. 12.)

Now sew in bridle ties to hold the stuffing (see page 31). The fibre or hair is picked over and passed under these ties, a handful at a time. Try to make sure it is spread evenly and compactly over the seat, $1\frac{1}{2}$ to 2 inches deep. Pack the fibre a little more closely along the front edge as this is to be stitched. This is not an easy part of the work, though in the view of some craftsmen it is the most important. It requires a great deal of patience and a sense of 'feel'.

Scrim should be placed over the stuffing and temporarily tacked into position with $\frac{1}{2}$ inch tacks. It is helpful to keep the thread of the scrim straight from front to back and from side to side. To assist in this, and also to keep the stuffing in place, stuffing ties should be stabbed through with a straight needle long enough to go right through the seat – possibly 16 inches long –

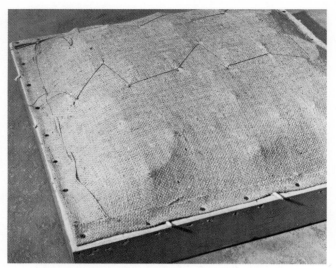

Fig. 12. Springs covered with hessian and partly sewn in.

and twine. At a point 6 or 7 inches from the front and close to the side of the seat push the needle down through the scrim, stuffing and hessian and then at a point roughly $\frac{3}{4}$ of an inch away, return the needle back up. Knot the twine and pull firmly. Now, with a free running twine stab through the seat at about 6 inch intervals over the area. (See Fig. 13.)

The front edge of the seat must now be prepared for stitching and this is very much a matter of practice. The stuffing must be adjusted to a sufficient firmness, more being added under the scrim as required. The temporary tacks holding the scrim can be removed and replaced once or twice at this stage. When you are satisfied that all is even, the scrim should be turned under and tacked down along the rasped edge with $\frac{3}{8}$ inch tacks. Along the edge an even line of thread in the scrim should be followed. (If the chair has a bowed or serpentine rail, initiative will have to be exercised to

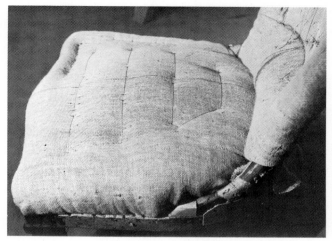

FIG. 13. Seat in scrim, showing stuffing ties in position.

keep a regular thickness of stuffing).

You are now ready to start stitching and will need a regulator, a 10 inch straight bayonet-pointed needle and twine. Commence with a blind stitch low down on the scrim, a short space above the tack line, and keep it level. Next, make the top stitch, or roll stitch. This is brought through the top of the scrim and forms a roll. The regulator is used to hook forward the stuffing as required. As progress is made the final firm line of the roll edge develops, of an even height and thickness – we hope. (See Fig. 14.)

The scrim at the back and sides should now be tacked down, the stuffing adjusted as necessary, and a smooth line achieved at the join of the arm and the back.

Bridle ties strung over the scrim surface receive the second stuffing – hair for preference – spread evenly and closely and of a full inch in thickness.

Calico should now be set over the hair, tacked temporarily and firmly strained. Then, commencing at

39

FIG. 14. Blind stitch completed and top stitch in progress, showing twist of twine round needle.

the centre of the front, take out the tacks in groups and strain the calico into position, moulding the line and shape of the edge as you go. Tack finally on the front of the rail. The back and sides should be tacked off and the domed effect of the seat contour should develop as work proceeds. Where necessary, the calico should be neatly cut and fitted round the upright members of the frame.

The old cover must now be replaced, with a layer or two of wadding set over the calico beneath. Temporary tacks will hold the cover in place while you fit it around the frame where the cutting was previously done. Then tack off permanently, along the underneath of the frame on the front and on top of the base rail on sides and back.

If the chair is up-turned once more it will facilitate the replacing of the outside arm cover and outside back cover. A piece of hessian tacked over the bottom of the chair, neatly turned in all round, will complete the repair.

Re-webbing the seat. Occasionally it is sufficient to replace the old webbing with new, so long as the webbing is fixed to the bottom of the chair frame, which is usual with a sprung seat.

Turn the chair upside down and rip off the bottom canvas. Release the covering, which will be tacked to the frame. The old webs will now be exposed. Remove the tacks which hold them and then cut away the twines which hold the webbing to the springs. (At this stage, inspect the springs to ensure that the lashings are intact and the hessian unbroken. If, at this stage, you decide that an entire new seat is necessary, turn back to the instructions given earlier in this chapter).

Generally one can put on the same number of webs as were removed. Fold over an end of the webbing and tack it to one end of the front rail with four or five $\frac{5}{8}$ inch tacks. Strain it to the back rail and secure it with 3 tacks. Cut the webbing, allowing $1\frac{1}{2}$ inches to fold back and fix with 2 more tacks. Continue until the requisite number of webs are fixed, each one being its own width away from the next. Now fix the webs which run across the chair, interlacing them with those you have already secured in place. (See page 30.)

It is helpful to fix some of the webs and then, putting your hands through the webbing, manipulate the springs into position and sew them to the webbing as you go. When the first row of springs has been sewn in place in this way, further webs can be placed and a second row of springs sewn and so on. The advantage of this procedure is that there is more freedom to adjust the springs and sew them to the webbing than if you wait until all the webbing is in place.

Finally, replace the cover edges and tack on a bottom canvas.

Re-upholstering a cushion-seated chair. The seat of this type of chair has a flat platform with a raised lip which allows the cushion to fit snugly into place. The early stages of the work are the same as those described in the first part of this chapter on re-upholstering an easy chair. Webbing and springing are done normally, although a special attempt should be made to lash the springs to a level flatness.

At the stuffing stage, the filling on the front of the seat has to be full in contrast to that on the centre (the platform) which should be lightly stuffed and flat. The necessary stitches are put in and the roll made (see page 40).

Now measure back from the front roll a margin of 5 or $5\frac{1}{2}$ inches and draw a line across using tailors chalk or a heavy pencil.

A piece of calico, long enough to tack at the sides and wide enough to sew on to the cane edge of a sprung-edge, or to tack under the frame of a firm-edge, should be pinned along the marked line with $\frac{1}{2}$ an inch or so turned under. It is probably best to use skewers with tacks at each end.

STITCHED IN WITH TWINE THROUGH
STUFFING

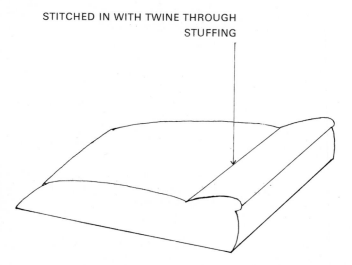

Fig. 15. Exposed seat, showing lipping profile and platform for cushion seat.

FIG. 16. Tub chair, showing sewn in lip of seat below cushion.

With a 14 inch needle draw twine up and down through the seat, tying the calico in on the scrim, taking the twine right through the spring hessian and back again. Finally, pull the twine tight, making a slight gutter, and tie it off. Pick some hair along the edge and pull the calico over it, either sewing it to the cane or tacking it under the frame, according to which type of frame you are working with. This creates the raised lip and the flat platform for the cushion to rest on (see Fig. 15). When the top cover is prepared for such a seat a strong tape, about $\frac{3}{4}$ of an inch wide, should be machine-stitched onto the underside in a line to marry

43

up with the calico lip.

Now, either stitch the tape on in a similar manner to that described above, or use a circular needle. Having put the wadding in place, draw the cover over the front and tack or sew it down. Tack the platform to the rail.

Spring edge work. A number of seats are built up with an independent spring edge. Such a built up edge adds to the general resilient comfort of the seat.

The usual practice is first to web the frame on the underside and then stand it on its feet. Now, fix 4 springs on top of the front rail. The best spring size for this work is 8 inch by 10 gauge, but this will, of course, vary according to the required height of the edge. If available, wire staples will hold the springs in place – 4 staples to each spring, set equidistant along the rail, leaving a clearance of one inch at each end from the arm upright. An alternative way to fix the springs is to use $\frac{5}{8}$ inch tacks and a strip of webbing, placing 2 tacks, one each side of the coil, at 4 points round the base.

The next stage is to tie these springs down to a predetermined height, in this case $8\frac{1}{2}$ inches from the bottom edge of the rail. Short pieces of webbing should be folded and laced around the narrow waist of the spring, the 2 ends splayed and tacked down to the required height. This will bring the spring forward and tilt it to the front, so to square it up again knot a piece of laid cord to the bottom coil at the rear of the spring. Take the cord up to a coil midway up the spring and knot it, pulling the rear of the spring down and bringing

FIG. 17. Plan of spring edge, showing cane turned at right angles and bound.

the top coil back to a level position. Continue the cord up to the top coil and knot again. Carry out this operation at each spring.

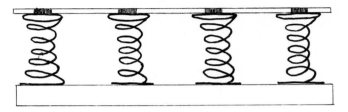

FIG. 18. Spring edge; front view.

Next, a length of upholsterers cane has to be tied to the springs, bound with twine. The two ends should be turned at right angles twice, (see Fig. 17).

The cane lies on top of the spring coil and is tied firmly with a series of looped knots. (A heavy gauge wire is sometimes used instead of cane, but cane is easier to work with.) See Fig. 18.

Other springs should now be sewn onto the webbing, in the centre of the seat. 10 inch by 9 gauge is generally the best for this.

The next process is to lash (tie) the springs together with laid cord. Initially, if a spring is pressed down by hand it has a light resistance until one feels a sort of hard core. It is to this hard core level that the spring is tied down. (In any case, on a spring edge seat, these centre springs should be tied down to the same level as the edge springs which are already fixed). First knot the cord and then tack it with a $\frac{5}{8}$ inch tack on top of the base rail. Carry it up to the third coil of the spring and knot it, continue it to the top coil and knot it, take it through to the top coil of the next spring, then to the third spring and then down and over the base rail on the opposite side of the chair. A return end of the cord, from the rail to the top of the spring, ties the top coil in position. Lashings should be made from side to side of

45

the chair and from back to front, making 4 knots on each spring. It is also advisable to tie the springs through the centre – the narrow waist coils – particularly on springs of 8 inches high or more. This will improve stability and give longer wear and is included in the best work.

Be very sure, when you tie down the springs, that they are upright. If they are not they will cripple or even snap in use and rapid deterioration of the seat will be the result. In this operation, it is essential that a knot is made at contact with the spring, and a clove hitch is recommended.

Hessian of at least 12 ounces in weight should be put over the springs. When cutting the hessian allow enough

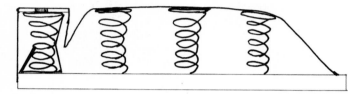

FIG. 19. View of spring seat, showing gutter.

to cover the seat and also to fold over for a second row of tacks. On the measure from front to back you must allow an additional 6 or 7 inches for the 'gutter' behind the front edge springs (see Fig. 19).

Starting with the back rail, centre the hessian, fold over $\frac{1}{2}$ an inch or so and tack securely with $\frac{1}{2}$ inch improved tacks. Now pull the hessian over the front and put in several temporary tacks at the front and sides. Pull the hessian taut. Next, release the front tacks and tuck the hessian down behind the front row of springs, making a gutter of perhaps 4 inches in depth. This gutter must be tied down, so stitch through a length (about 6 feet) of laid cord along this bottom fold of the hessian. You must now draw a loop of cord between each pair of front edge springs and tack each loop firmly on the front rail with a $\frac{5}{8}$ inch tack, twisting the cord around the tack. This will give you the necessary ditch between the front edge springs and the seat springs.

Take the hessian back over the cane and, again, tack it temporarily. You will be left with a bunch of hessian by the arm upright part of the frame and this must be cut and fitted. Fold back and cut with care, allowing the gutter to follow through just behind the arm rail and neatly box in the end spring, making a fold down the front corner.

Using a spring needle and twine, sew the hessian to the cane. Loop the twine around the cane, making a blanket stitch at intervals of an inch or so. The hessian at the sides can now receive its final tacks. Release the tacks on the front edge and tack off to an even height on the front of the rail. Sew in the seat springs (see page 36).

Bridle ties should now be sewn over the seat at 6 inch intervals and the fibre or hair picked in (see page 31). First, push some stuffing into the gutter, filling it well and firmly, and then fill in around the back and sides, below the tacking rails. Continue working forwards, tucking the fibre under the twine loops, picking it over and fluffing it up to an even density of about one and a half inches.

It is not easy to decide just how firmly to stuff the chair at this stage – only practice or experience will really tell you how much fibre or hair you need. Along the front edge, make the stuffing quite firm.

Scrim should be put over the filling. When cutting the scrim, allow an extra inch on the sides and back to tack down and 3 or 4 inches on the front (where a roll will be stitched).

Temporarily tack the scrim on to the base rail of the frame but, as you cannot tack on to the cane, the front edge must be held in place with skewers. Draw the scrim over the edge and pierce a skewer through scrim and hessian, just under the cane. Use a downward, curled movement and the skewer will hold. Only thrust just far enough for the skewer to hold or it will come up through the top of the scrim. Put in skewers about 4 inches apart and pull just enough to clear away any slackness.

Now insert stuffing ties (see page 39). Use a straight, bayonet pointed needle. In this case, a needle 14 inches long will be needed because of the overall thickness of the seat. Thread a length of twine of about 6 feet long. About 7 inches back from the cane and 4 inches from the side rail push the needle down through the stuffing, springs and webbing. Get a grip of the needle below the webbing, pull it through sufficiently to clear the hessian, and then return the needle back up through the stuffing from a point about $\frac{3}{4}$ of an inch away from the point of entry. Make a slip knot and tie down. From this point, at intervals of 6 inches, repeat the process over the whole area of the seat, except that the twine should now be run through without knots until the last tie is in place, when the twine should be pulled taut and tied off.

Attention should now be turned to the front edge. As it is not possible to tack on to the cane, everything must be sewn on. Pull out a couple of skewers and adjust the stuffing – most likely a little fibre will need to be added. Turn the edge of the scrim under and, with the skewers, pin along the front of the cane. Next, sew the scrim to the hessian using a circular needle and twine, making sure that the stitch is made through the hessian on the cane or just below. What is known as a blind stitch is now set along the edge. Use a 10 inch straight, bayonet pointed needle and, starting at the left of the seat, pierce the scrim immediately above the cane and draw the needle out at the top of the seat about 5 inches back. Without pulling the needle right through, return it to a point about 2 inches from the previous point of departure and make a slip knot. At intervals of 2 inches repeat the action, twisting the twine twice around the needle and pulling it firm each time.

This first stitch draws the stuffing forwards in preparation for the top stitch. The top, or roll, stitch makes a firm edge and shape to the seat. Using the same needle, pierce in close above the blind stitch and, keeping the needle at an almost upright angle, stitch right through, so forming a roll of about an inch in diameter. If necessary, use the regulator to adjust the stuffing so that the roll is of a consistant firmness. Provided the scrim has been sewn on to the cane to an even thread, a similar line can be followed when stitching, making the work somewhat easier. The scrim along the sides and back should then be tacked home, the surplus tucked underneath and tacked through the double thickness.

Stitch in bridle ties and fill in with hair, not too thickly but evenly. Spread over a piece of calico and temporarily tack it into place, using skewers along the front. Strain it down firmly and sew it to the cane line along the front. Tack it along the back and sides.

Lay wadding on the calico and secure the final cover, sewn along the front and tacked down tightly at the sides. $\frac{1}{2}$ inch tacks will probably be necessary at this stage because by now there are several thicknesses of material on the rail.

A sprung edge seat of this type has to be finished with a border. Cut the material to the right size and lay the chair on its back on the floor. Fold the top edge of the material under and pin it along the cane line. Then lay the material back on to the seat. Put some bridle ties in on the hessian along this front border and fill in with hair. Lay wadding over the hair, bring the cover back over and tack it into place under the frame. Each end of this front border must be tidied up. The seat cover should be pulled down at the sides, tacked to the bottom rail, taken over on to the hessian and stitched. The border cover should be turned in, pinned to the seat material and slip stitched.

Always remember that the spring edges must be free; if attached to the arm upright or the arm they would not be free to rise and fall and the top cover would tear when the chair was sat on.

Spring units. In some instances the seat of a chair is built up on a spring unit, designed with either a single or a double layer of springs.

49

D

FIG. 20. Spring unit with single core springs.

If there is anything wrong with the spring unit itself it will have to be dispensed with because these units cannot be repaired successfully. However, problems are likely to arise in trying to obtain a replacement. Each unit is designed for a particular model and by the time re-upholstery becomes necessary the model is likely to be obsolete. A new unit can be made if a spring maker can be contracted – but this is usually a matter of trade contact, difficult for the private individual to arrange, and expensive in the case of a single unit.

Fortunately, it is likely that the unit will be in quite good condition and that all that is necessary is for the seat to be re-upholstered.

Part of the work is done on these units before they are fixed to the frame, so your first job is to strip the chair down and detach the unit. Cut a piece of hessian to cover the top of the unit, allowing about 12 inches extra all round – sufficient to tack down on the base rail. Skewer the hessian in position and then, with a spring needle and twine, stitch it to the wire edge of the unit.

50

Cut a piece of scrim 4 inches larger than the top frame and skewer it down. Mark a line 5 inches in from the wire edge on all 4 sides. Using a circular needle, sew the scrim to the hessian along this line with a running twine.

Remove the skewers and push hair or fibre under the free scrim. Turn the scrim ends under and skewer them to the wire edge, thus making a padded border around the seat of about 2 inches in thickness. This can now be stitched in place with a combination blind stitch. Use a 12 inch bayonet pointed needle. Insert the needle immediately above the wire on the edge, take it up into the stuffing about 5 inches back and work it back again to come out below the wire edge. Make a slip knot and pull tight. Now, at intervals of 2 inches, pierce above the wire and return below the wire, twist the twine twice round the needle and pull firmly.

A stitched roll can now be sewn along the front. (See page 40.)

At this stage the spring unit should be fixed into the frame. It will be fairly obvious how this should be done. The clips along the front should be secured with clout nails and the metal straps (webs) stretched and fixed to the frame.

When the unit is in position the hessian should be tacked down very tightly with $\frac{1}{2}$ inch tacks on top of the rail – the surplus should be cut away leaving an inch to fold over and tack again. The usual sequence is now followed – bridle ties are sewn in on the top surface of the scrim and hair is picked in to form a nicely domed seat; calico is placed over and sewn in under the roll edge, with sides and back tacked on to the base rail. A layer of wadding and the cover should now be applied – sewn to the front and tacked around to form a smooth edge and a clean-lined seat contour.

In some designs the seat cover will be all in one and will be taken right over the front edge and tacked under the frame. In others the seat cover stops at the seat edge – in this case a border cover should be pinned along under the edge, bridle ties and hair stuffing put in, wadding laid over and the border cover brought down under the frame and tacked.

Upholstering arms and back. The re-upholstering of a chair seat has already been described above – chair arms and backs are built up on similar principles.

As always, stripping down is the first job, treating the top cover carefully if you intend to replace it.

Springs can be attached to chair arm rails in one of two ways – you can either staple them in place or slip a short length of webbing over the bottom loop of each spring and tack the webbing to the chair rail. Tie each spring to the arm rail, using cord, and reducing the height of the springs by perhaps an inch. Next, cover the whole with hessian, pick over the hair stuffing, tack scrim overall and stitch any roll edges as required (see page 40); all as described above in the directions given for the renewing of the chair seat.

Patience and care must be exercised at this stage if the arms are shaped or have scrolls along the front. To form these shapes, fullness in the scrim will have to be adjusted, gathered neatly and tacked down. Now insert the bridle ties and pick in the stuffing to the height and firmness required. Finish with a calico covering, tightly placed, and the top cover. Finally, the 'facing' piece of arm cover must be pinned into place, with a thin layer of wadding underneath, and slip stitched neatly to the top arm cover.

Chair backs should be webbed in the same manner as the seats and 11 or 12 gauge springs (lighter than those used in seats) sewn into place. These springs should be tied into position with twine rather than laid cord, and hessian pulled over. Hair stuffing should then be picked in; the edges tacked down and stitched to the desired size and contour of the chair back. The second stuffing and the cover complete the job.

Outside arms and back are usually lined with hessian to add some support to the top cover. Tack it tautly to enclose the webbing and any other visible parts of the upholstery. The top edges can be back tacked, the cover pulled firmly into place and tacked under the frame, and

FIG. 21. Arm cover cut in under back; see also tacking under rail.

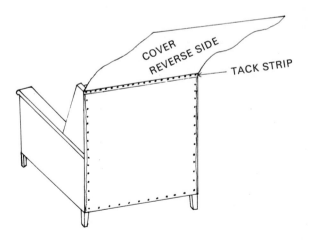

FIG. 22. Back tacking.

the sides neatly turned in and pinned into place preparatory to slip stitching. Gimp pins may be used
instead of slip stitching if you prefer.

Back tacking. This is frequently done on outside
backs and outside arms. See Fig. 22. The cover material
must be cut an inch larger all round than the size of the
frame. With the back of the chair facing you, and the
wrong side of the material towards you, tack the material to the frame. Next, close tack a strip of webbing
about half an inch wide along the top rail. Now bring
the cover back over, strain it down and tack it to the
bottom rail. The sides can be slip stitched.

The Panel-Backed Chair

These chairs have an exposed framework – which may be polished, painted or gilded – around the upholstered centre of the back. On some period chairs, the arms are made up in the same way, and in either case the treatment is the same.

Work on these chairs should ideally be skilled, and you will certainly need great patience and a realisation of the lightweight and delicate nature of the frame. It is advisable, for instance, to have a supporting block underneath the rail on which you are hammering – even perhaps going to the trouble of making a felt-covered, shaped cradle to protect the surface of the frame.

All tacking has to be done on a rebated edge on the inside of the frame. This edge is frequently only $\frac{3}{4}$ of an inch wide, or less. Always use a cabriole hammer for this type of work.

Great care must be taken, when ripping off the old materials, that the framework does not suffer damage, because it is exposed to the rear as well as to the front. Any unfortunate splitting, scratching, etc., will have to be put right before upholstering commences. In fact, should the whole frame be scheduled for repolishing and renovation, this should be done prior to upholstering.

In this instance, the first piece of material to be fixed is the outside back covering, which should be cut at least one inch larger all round than the panel back.

FIG. 23. Panel backed
chair; front view.

FIG. 24. Panel backed
chair; rear view.

With the chair facing you, and the wrong side of the material towards you (so that the right side appears on the back of the chair) tack the material carefully to the rebate inside the frame. Use $\frac{1}{4}$ inch fine tacks if possible, although $\frac{3}{8}$ inch fine tacks will do. Improved tacks are too heavy for this work. Use just sufficient number of tacks to hold the material in place. With a sharp knife, carefully cut away any surplus material.

Your next job is to build up the panel towards you until it is smoothly padded and ready to receive its top cover.

First apply a thin layer of wadding. Now cut a piece of hessian about $\frac{3}{4}$ of an inch larger, all round, than required. Tack it into place with $\frac{3}{8}$ inch fine tacks, fold back the surplus $\frac{3}{4}$ of an inch and tack again. Within reason, use as few tacks as possible.

Cut a piece of scrim at least 2 inches larger than the panel all round. Tack it temporarily to the rebate. Now mark a chalk line 2 inches in from the inside edge of the frame, following the shape of the panel to be worked on. Using a circular needle, sew the scrim to the hessian, close in to the frame, following the chalk line. Use a running twine – one with no knots except at the beginning and end of the sewing.

Now release the tacks in groups and fill in with stuffing under the free scrim. You should aim to achieve a roll about $1\frac{1}{2}$ inches high, replacing the temporary tacks as you go. Adjust the stuffing until it is even and firm and tack down tidily, taking care that the tacks are properly placed and are not breaking the frame edge below, out of sight.

You are now at the stage illustrated in Figure 25c.

Stitching up the roll, to make it neat and sharp, calls for a 6 inch circular needle rather than a straight needle because of the risk of scratching the frame surface. One row of blind stitching is sewn in low down, close to the tacks, and then a top stitch, making a sharp roll.

You have now to fill in the hollow centre of the panel, up to the level of the top of the roll. String in bridle ties and pick in hair stuffing to an even level (see page 31).

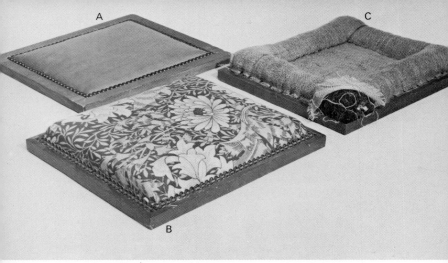

FIG. 25. Panels for chair backs with show-wood edges.
  a) Pincushion style of upholstery, covered with hide and close nailed.
  b) Covered and finished with gimp.
  c) Part upholstered preparatory to stitching.

Tack a piece of calico over the whole.

The front cover, cut $\frac{1}{2}$ an inch larger all round, can now be set on top of the calico and tacked carefully into place, the edges turned under neatly, close to the show wood edge of the rebate.

The tacks will be exposed, and gimp will give a tidy finish (see Fig. 25b).

CHAPTER EIGHT

Leatherwork

The term leather usually refers to cowhide but other skins, such as goat and sheep, are also used in upholstery and the techniques involved are the same, as indeed they are for imitation leathers, plastic-coated cloths and plastic materials.

See page 26 for advice on estimating the quantity of hide required for a particular job. Always bear in mind that the best quality material is to be found in the centre of the hide, along the backbone.

Hide, in its way, is heavier and harder to handle than woven materials. The stuffing in a leather-covered chair should be built up more firmly and packed more tightly than the stuffing in a chair destined for a softer covering. It is definitely helpful to cover the chair completely with calico before beginning to work with the leather covering.

The hide should be set on and temporarily tacked into position. It must be strained really tightly because hide has a great deal of stretch in itself. To achieve the proper tautness of covering, the temporary tacking will have to be repeated two or three times. Release each tack separately, strain the hide a fraction more, and tack again. Only put in the final tacks when you are satisfied that the hide has been pulled sufficiently tightly.

Exposed corners, pleats and joins are often hand-slipped on soft, woven materials, but on hide this is not possible. Therefore, on sections where pleats and joins are involved, the hide cover should be set in position on each section of the chair and 'tailored' by cutting and fitting the joins and shaping as necessary. Then the cover section should be removed, machine stitched, reset on the seat, arm or wherever, and tacked down. This 'tailoring' procedure will be necessary chiefly on the seat, arms and inside back of the chair. The outside arms and the back must be finished off along the edges; these should be turned in and tacked with gimp pins, which will be virtually invisible, or with antique brass nails for show.

In certain types of leather-upholstered work the 'look' is soft and loose. In these cases, whether you are renovating or completely re-covering, there is no need to strain and stretch the hide; the cover can be set on easily. You must, of course, select your covering material accordingly, choosing softer hide for the loose look.

CHAPTER NINE

Buttoning and Trimming

Upholstery button-work really requires some experience and should be attempted only when some proficiency has been attained at the simpler work.

Preparation is of primary importance. The build-up and shaping of, say, a buttoned chair back entails quite a degree of care and affects not only the facility of working but also the final results.

If you are restoring a piece of furniture the old cover and at least some of the buttons will, of course, be *in situ*, and they will be a guide when planning the new covering. When you come to mark the positions for the new buttons it is important to understand that the groundwork markings – that is, the markings on the undercovering surface – are of one size and the cover markings of a different size, to allow for the pleating of the cover material. Figure 26 will give an impression of what is needed.

First remove the old cover, taking out tacks where necessary and cutting the twine ties which hold the buttons. The hair and wadding stuffing will now be exposed and, providing it is in reasonable condition and shape, can be left undisturbed and re-buttoned with a fair prospect of success.

Once the cover is off, measurements can be taken of the vertical and horizontal distances between buttons, using for guidance the marks left on the old cover and the ends of the twine ties protruding from the old stuffing.

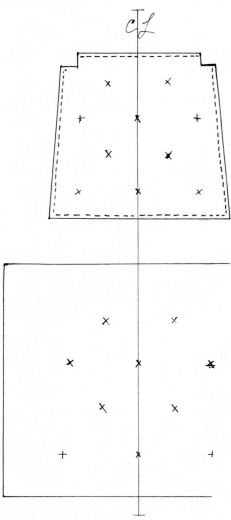

F<small>IG</small>. 26. Buttoning
Top: Groundwork marking on scrim.
Bottom: Cover marking.

Spread the new cover material face downwards on a cutting board or table. With tailors chalk, draw a line down the centre. From this central line, mark the appropriate points where the buttons are to go. When transferring measurements from the old cover to the new, remember that the old cover is almost certainly distorted and stretched and therefore reduce all measures by a $\frac{1}{4}$ of an inch.

It is particularly in this sort of work – re-covering and re-buttoning a whole area – that experience shows, because it is not at all easy to be sure that the measures are correct. For one thing, especially on shaped chair backs, buttons may be fixed wider apart or closer to on different levels. Also, the type of cover material used has to be taken into consideration because flexibility and stretch can have a bearing on how the pleats fall into place.

The buttons themselves must be stamped out from the cover material by a trimming maker (a local upholsterer or furniture shop should be able to give you an address); you cannot make them yourself.

Equip yourself with a straight buttoning needle with a fine point of 10 inches long, a regulator, scissors and some strong, fine twine. Spread a layer of wadding over the existing stuffing and break a hole through it where each button is to go. Thread a length of twine through a button, put both ends of the twine through the eye of the needle, and pierce the top cover (right side towards you), making sure that you know which mark on the cover relates to which mark on the chair, and always beginning near the centre of the area. Pass the needle right through the stuffing to the outside back, pulling the button down into the hollow. Make a slip knot on the twine, insert a tuft (a scrap piece of calico or hessian) and pull the twine tight. Leave a length of several inches, and cut.

Continue in this way with the other buttons. Presuming that you are working on diamond buttoning, it is advisable to complete one diamond at a time, progressively folding the pleats into place with the help of the flat end of the regulator. All pleats fold downwards and are set diagonally.

The pleats will not necessarily fall easily into place, and you will have to manipulate the folds with the flat end of the regulator, adjust the stuffing with its point, and possibly work below the cover (which is not yet tacked down) to improve the appearance

When the diamonds in the centre are completed, turn your attention to the outside edges, where the cover is to be taken over the edge and tacked to the frame. At this stage the pleats may well be pulled over vertically or horizontally as opposed to the diagonal setting of the others. A deciding factor will be the shape of the chair back. A square or straight-line effect would indicate vertical and horizontal pleats, whereas in the case of a rounded effect the pleats can be taken over in any direction which gives a pleasing effect, bearing in mind that both sides must be balanced.

Those pleats at the bottom of the back, leading onto the seat, must always go straight down, be carried through to the back rail and tacked.

When the buttoning is finished the cover must be tacked down. It will be necessary to put in temporary tacks several times until the cover is set correctly. Then the final tacks can be put in.

Now return to the button twines. Pull the buttons down tightly and tie off the knot securely.

In the work described above one was making use of the existing stuffing. If, however, the back has to be re-stuffed the process is somewhat different.

The chair back should be stripped down to the frame, webbed as necessary and hessian tacked over.

A central, vertical line should be marked on the hessian with tailors chalk and the positions of the buttons marked in.

You will need fine twine, a straight buttoning needle and some odd cuttings of calico or hessian for tufts.

From the front of the chair, pierce the needle and twine through a button mark to the back. Fold up a scrap tuft, take the needle and twine through that, and return through the hessian from the back to the front.

Cut the twine, leaving two ends of about 10 inches each. Lightly knot these together and leave. Repeat this operation at each button mark, taking the twine through the webbing if that is what the mark demands.

Next, sew in bridle ties for the stuffing (see page 31), tuck hair stuffing under and pick it in all over the back. Work the hair in evenly, fully 2 inches thick, allowing it the full freedom of its springy nature. As you proceed, bring the button ties up through the stuffing. Place wadding over the hair and break through it to draw the button twines up.

Positions of the buttons should now be marked on the wrong side of the top cover (bearing in mind the points made earlier).

Buttoning and folding now proceeds as outlined above.

I must stress again that work of this nature requires a great deal of patience and a lot of fingering and manipulating to obtain a satisfactory result.

Float or star buttoning is achieved by a simpler procedure. The top cover is fitted and tacked on. Next, a buttoning needle is stabbed through at pre-determined places with button and twine attached. The twine ends are tied into a slip knot, a tuft slid inside, and the knot

FIG. 27. Deep buttoning (right) and float buttoning.

pulled tight. This can be done on seat, arms and back, as desired.

To replace a single button is not always a simple repair. If the fault is a broken twine, and the button to hand, it simply needs to be tied in again.

If the button is broken or missing you will need a replacement. It is expensive to have a single button made and you will also be faced with the problem of finding a small piece of the original cover material. However, if the chair is a good or favourite one it is worth the effort and cost. If you open the bottom canvas of the chair (or sofa) you may well find a surplus piece of material to take to the trimming maker.

Thread a fine-pointed buttoning needle with fine twine and thrust it through at the point where the button is missing. Be very careful not to tear the cover. You will feel the needle work its way through the stuffing until it emerges at the back, Now return it to the front, from a point $\frac{1}{2}$ an inch away, so that you create an anchorage for the pull of the twine. If there are springs to be negotiated, be sure to avoid looping the twine around a spring coil. Thread the button, make a slip knot, draw the button into place and tie securely. Cut the surplus twine and tuck the ends under the button with the blunt end of the regulator.

You may feel it necessary to open up the outside back or outside arm for a sufficient distance to give you freedom to operate. If you do this, the button can then be threaded on the twine, stabbed through from the front and knotted at the back. You must now replace the outside back or arm in the manner of its initial attachment – either by hand slip-stitching with a circular needle and linen thread or by means of gimp pins.

Replacing the buttons in a cushion is a simple task, so long as you have the buttons for replacement. Using a smooth-pointed buttoning-needle, thread a button onto twine and take it through the cushion at the required spot. Thread on the second button, for the other side, make a slip knot, draw firmly and tie off securely. Cut the surplus twine and tuck the ends beneath the second button.

Replacing a button in a headboard is also quite straightforward. Headboards are usually made of ply-board and a hole will have been bored through the board behind each button. The twine can thus be drawn through the hole and tacked on the rear. Some head-boards are framed with a webbing and hessian centre. In this case the buttoning can be done in the simpler way of stabbing the needle through the hessian. In either case, it will almost certainly be necessary to open the lining on the back of the headboard to do a neat job.

Trimmings, in upholstery work, are used not only to add decoration and colour but also to conceal tacks, especially those holding down the cover on show-wood furniture. Gimp, braid, fringe and cord are often used in this way and occasionally fringe is used to hide chair legs (in which case it should clear the floor by about $\frac{1}{2}$ an inch).

Gimp, or braid, is probably the easiest trimming to fix. It can be stuck down with Copydex, although any proprietary brand of glue will do, so long as it is suitable for adhesion to fabric.

Make a start at the edge, by a leg. First fold an end under and drive in a temporary tack. Spread the adhesive as advised on the tube, not too thickly, over an area of about 12 inches. Press the braid or gimp into place and insert temporary tacks at intervals to hold it until the glue has dried and set. Gently tapping the braid with a hammer ensures a firm fix. When adhesion is complete, remove the temporary tacks. Next, insert some gimp pins, $\frac{3}{8}$ of an inch, at 4 inch intervals, and especially on shaped edges. The heads of these pins should be carefully hidden in the weave of the braid.

Fringe can be fixed in the same way, although it is traditionally correct to sew the fringe heading to the fabric cover.

Leather or plastic coverings require different treatment. Adhesives are not satisfactory. Brass-headed nails, obtainable in a variety of surface finishes, are frequently used on an edge and give a pleasing effect. On show wood, if you are trying to conceal the edges of hide and tacks, the brass-headed nails should be close-set, side by side. If used purely for decoration, you can space them evenly along the line of the frame.

Another method is to use banding and studs. A strip $\frac{1}{2}$ an inch wide of leather, imitation leather or PVC is fixed in position with brass-headed nails or with studs (tacks covered as buttons to match the covering on the chair).

It is recommended that that part of the frame into which the nails are to be driven be examined to see that the wood is reasonably sound. Should the frame be very much pitted with old tack holes, a coating of scotch glue or even plastic wood will give a better holding quality to the wood.

PART TWO

Mending and Restoring Soft Furnishings

CHAPTER TEN

Assessing the Problems

These days, so many things can combine to make soft furnishings look tatty and neglected. Curtains and loose covers are expensive items, requiring quite a yardage of cloth and quite a lot of skill and time to produce first class results, so it is in the interests of economy as well as aesthetics to give them the care they deserve.

The pollution from passing traffic penetrates into window curtains; cigarette smoke and cooking smells may abound inside the house. Curtains also tend to fade on the edges exposed to strong light, and their inner edges become worn by continual hand closing. Curtain linings fade and split. Loose covers become faded, worn and soiled by accidental spillage, or marred with cigarette burns, or perhaps they shrink during laundering or cleaning. Eiderdowns become worn on the outer edges or the top cover fades. The trailing ends of bedcovers can be ripped. Down cushions may require new inner cases. Pelmets lose their crisp, tailored lines after repeated cleaning.

Or perhaps a change of residence may mean that some alterations have to be made to otherwise usable soft furnishings.

All these problems can be overcome so long as you have the time and patience to tackle the work.

Some materials must be treated with more respect than others, and I have tried to make this clear in the relevant chapters. For instance, the making of articles in velour or velvet requires the utmost care. Never tear velour because the torn edge will contract and the weave of the threads tighten and distort the fabric for the depth of several inches.

The usual practice, when velour is made into curtains, is to have the pile running downwards – that is, from the heading to the bottom of the hem – unless a brighter shade of colour is desired, in which case you can reverse this procedure.

When seaming velour, first pin the seams with steel dressmakers pins; reduce the pressure of the machine foot and make the stitch length 10 to an inch (2½ cm). Always machine down the pile, holding the velour taut without pulling or dragging.

If piping has to be made in velour or velvet, see that the pile on the covering for the cord runs in the same direction; a mistake will be very apparent. When hand sewing, cover the left hand (right hand if you are left handed) with a strip of velvet, to prevent sharp indents being made in the pile by the finger nails.

Chintz sometimes presents problems. It is often impossible to cut the lower edge of a curtain to pattern across the width and still have a lower edge that is straight and square. The only solution is to ignore the pattern and cut the curtains straight and square.

If, in the seaming of printed or woven fabrics, the pattern or motifs are too far out of true to match successfully for the length of the seam, for instance on curtains, match the seam at eye level and let it run out of true above and below this point. It is better to have a mis-matched seam than a puckered seam.

It is with all these points in mind that I have written the following chapters, hoping that they will help you to revitalise your own soft furnishings.

N.R.

CHAPTER ELEVEN

Equipment

The sewing machine
The domestic sewing machine is capable of handling most soft furnishings; the only doubtful jobs might be during the construction or repair of loose-covers, where one piped seam crosses another piped seam. At this point six thicknesses of fabric would be involved. Best to play it safe and sew together by hand.

Useful machine attachments are the zipper or half foot for the machining of piping cord, and the gathering foot for frills and flounces. If your machine has a swing needle action this will prove most helpful in the neatening of seams.

Fully automatic machines with a range of built-in embroidery stitches can be used to decorate and to camouflage seams on cushions, curtains and bedcovers.

Keep your sewing machine covered when not in use; store it in a heated room; clean and oil it regularly, but use oil sparingly. (Approx. £40 to £160 new.)

Scissors
A sharp pair of shears, 7 to 8 inches (18 to 20 cm) long, for the the cutting out of fabric. (£1.25)

A smaller pair of scissors, 4 to 5 inches (10 to 13 cm), long for ordinary use. (80p)

Never use your sewing scissors for cutting paper as this will blunt them.

Pins
1 inch ($2\frac{1}{2}$ cm) stainless steel dressmaking pins are ideal for general use. (22p)

Hand sewing needles

A selection of various sized sharps; fine for hemmings and slip stitching, thicker for the sewing on of curtain hooks etc. (7p per packet.)

Machine needles

Various sizes from fine No. 11 to the thicker No. 16. (3 for 10p.)

Threads

No. 40 sewing cottons for general use, and synthetic thread for man-made fabrics. (7p)

Button thread, which is a strong waxed linen, for the sewing on of curtain hooks and rings, or hooks and eyes or press studs on loose covers. (20p).

Rulers

An expanding metal rule up to 10 feet (3 metres) will make the accurate measurements of windows easier. (£1.50).

A small 6 inch (15 cm) rule will be found to be most useful during the pressing of hems and also when checking hems during machining, as the shortness of the rule enables it to pass under the machine head. (10p).

Tape measure

A good glass fibre measure which will not shrink or stretch, for measuring loose-cover sections and when taking measurements over bedclothes and pillows. (17p).

Tailors chalk

For indicating cutting lines. (4p).

Thimbles

It is impossible to hand sew soft furnishings without a thimble, many of the fabrics being thicker and heavier than dress fabrics. Never use a plastic thimble, as its surface is very slippery, causing the eye of the needle to 'skid off'. A painful, stabbed finger can be the result. Choose a strong metal thimble. (12p).

Pin-pad

Worn on the wrist, it can be purchased quite cheaply, or you can make your own. It is an invaluable aid, saving the necessity of constantly reaching for the pin box and leaving both hands free.

Electric iron

A heat controlled thermostatic dry or steam iron will

be needed for pressing, through various stages of remaking and repairing soft furnishings. (£6.50).

Note book

Keep a small note book especially for calculations. Much safer than writing some very necessary measurements on an odd piece of loose paper that can easily be mislaid.

A large table will be useful to spread curtains out to their full extent for cutting or reparing; use a dining table with extended top or else clear a floor space.

The prices of the above items vary from stockist to stockist, and may have risen since we went to press – they are offered as a general guide only.

CHAPTER TWELVE

Stitches and General Procedures

The principle hand-sewing stitches used in soft furnishing are the following:–
Tacking or basting stitches

FIG. 28a.

Uneven tacking or basting (Fig. 28A)
   Uneven tacking is worked from right to left, making a short underneath stitch and a long stitch on the top.

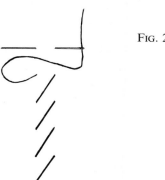

FIG. 28b.

77

Diagonal tacking or basting (Fig. 28B)

Work either way, from or towards yourself, depending on which is the most convenient.

Make a short stitch through the fabric pointing the needle to the left crossways. Continue to make another short stitch in the same manner about $1\frac{1}{2}$ inches (4 cm) from the first stitch. Keep the stitches in line and the result will be a short stitch underneath and a long diagonal on the surface.

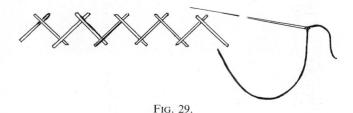

FIG. 29.

Herringbone (Fig. 29)

Work from left to right on an imaginary double line, the needle always pointing to the left. Pick up a piece of material alternatively, first on the hem at the lower line and then just directly above the hem.

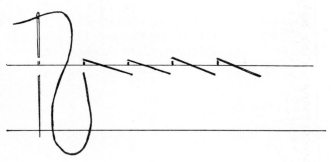

FIG. 30.

Serging (Fig. 30)

Work from right to left. Starting with a knot, bring the needle out from the edge of the single fold at about $\frac{1}{4}$ inch ($\frac{1}{2}$ cm) from the selvedge or raw edge. Insert the needle vertically about 1 inch (2 cm) further along so that the point is facing you, and pick up one or two threads of fabric at just above the fold, bringing the needle immediately through the fold below. Continue in this manner for the length required.

Fig. 31.

Locking (Fig. 31)

This is a large blanket stitch, used for holding together lining and face fabric. It is worked from left to right.

Insert the needle vertically through the fold on the extreme edge of the lining, only taking up one or two threads, and bring the needle immediately in to the face material, again picking up one or two threads. Make sure that the cotton is under the needle when the needle is pulled through. Make the next stitch from 4 to 6 inches (10 to 15 cm) along. Continue for the length required. Do not pull the cotton tight, but leave loose so that a loop of cotton exists between each stitch.

Open back-stitch (Fig. 32)

This stitch is worked from right to left. Make a back stitch through the fabric bringing the needle out $\frac{1}{4}$ inch ($\frac{1}{2}$ cm) further along. Make a back-stitch and again a space. Proceed for the length required.

Slip-stitch (Fig. 33)

When completed correctly this stitch should be

79

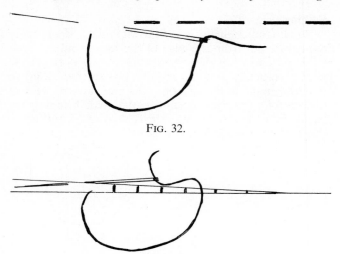

Fig. 32.

Fig. 33.

invisible. It is worked right to left, or towards you, depending on the article being made, and is used mostly for attaching linings.

Make a small stitch on the face fabric, i.e. on the margin of the face fabric right against the lining. Make a small stitch on the lining on the folded edge, making sure that the stitch on the lining is parallel with the stitch made on the face fabric. The stitches, when pulled apart, should resemble a ladder. Pull stitches together so that the fabric lies perfectly flat without puckering.

Slip-hemming (Fig. 34)

This is a combination of slipping and hemming, used

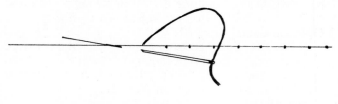

Fig. 34.

for sewing the hems of soft furnishings. It is worked from right to left. Catch a thread of fabric, then run the needle through the edge of the hem for about $\frac{1}{4}$ inch ($\frac{1}{2}$ cm); then repeat the process.

Piping

Piping, either in self or contrast fabric, is used as a decoration on chair covers, cushions, bedcovers, eiderdowns and as a pelmet edging. Piping cord can be obtained in various thicknesses, the most popular thickness being No. 2, with the finer No. 1 being used for eiderdowns.

Calculate the amount of cord required and wash before using; this will prevent distortion by shrinkage after the article is cleaned.

Piping cord is joined by splicing together the ends; cut allowing it to overlap $1\frac{1}{2}$ inches (4 cm). Piping cord has a three-core twist; untwist the two ends to be joined for a short distance. Cut two strands away on one piece and one strand on the other. Now twist the two ends together and bind with cotton.

Crossway strips

Crossway strips are used for the covering of piping cords. They are made as follows: Fold the cloth by taking one corner, as shown in diagram 35 to form a 45° angle. Cut out this fold, and continue cutting, at this angle, strips of cloth $1\frac{1}{2}$ inches (4 cm) wide for No. 2 piping, $1\frac{1}{4}$ inches (3 cm) wide for No. 1 piping, until enough strips are available to make the required length. (Fig. 36.) Join strips as shown. (Figs. 37 and 38.) Press seams open with a warm iron. Fold crossway around the cord and tack stitch as shown. (Fig. 39.) Clip at curved edges and corners as Fig. 40 and 41. Make final join as shown. (Diagram 42.)

Mitred corners

Mitred corners occur frequently in the making of soft furnishing. They present a neat way of eliminating bulk at a point where two hems meet. Mitres on curtains differ from those used in dressmaking, in that the excess is not trimmed away, but left, in case it should be necessary for the curtain to be lengthened.

81

F

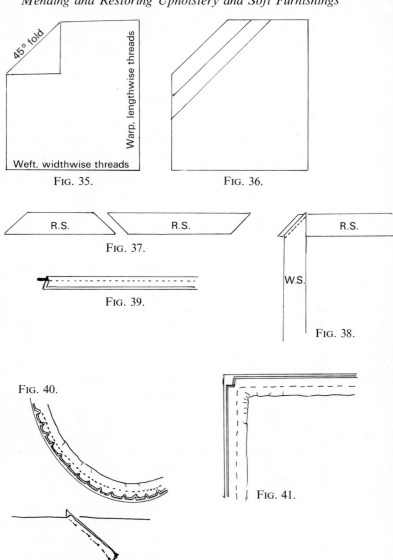

FIG. 35.

FIG. 36.

FIG. 37.

FIG. 39.

FIG. 38.

FIG. 40.

FIG. 41.

FIG. 42.

When slip-stitching a mitre, always work from the inner edge to the outer-edge.

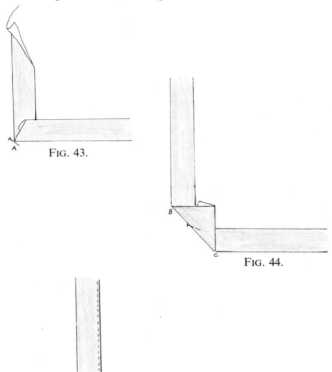

Fig. 43.

Fig. 44.

Fig. 45.

45° mitre with balanced hems

This is a mitre on a double hem, when both hems are of the same dimension. The procedure is as follows: Fold a double hem on each edge and press. Place a pin at point 'A'. (Fig. 43). Open one fold on each hem, so that there are only single turns each side. Make a

83

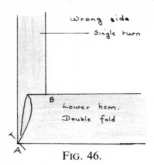

FIG. 46.

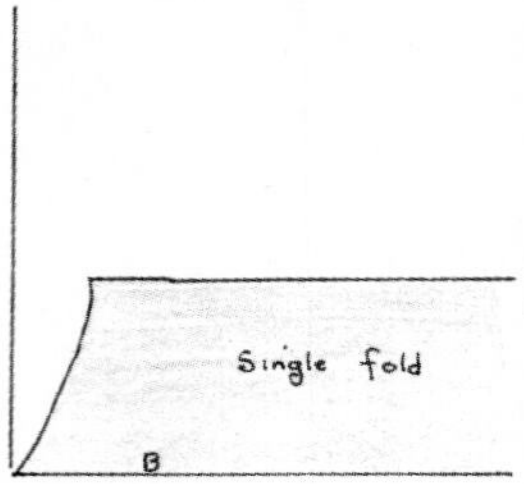

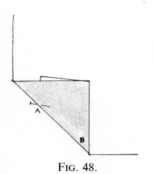

FIG. 47.

FIG. 48.

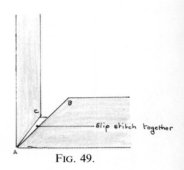

FIG. 49.

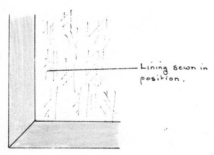

FIG. 50.

diagonal fold of 45°, keeping the pin on the edge of the fold. (Fig. 44). Fold 'B' and 'C' inwards to meet on the inside of the hem. Pin and slip-stitch. (Fig. 45.)

45° mitre with unbalanced hems

A 45° mitre is made on the lower edge of a curtain having a lining with a loose bottom.

Although the width of the side and bottom hem vary, when the lining is in place it shows a uniform margin of 1 inch (2½ cm). (Fig. 50.)

Proceed as follows:– Press the side and bottom for a single 1½ inches (4 cm). Press the bottom hem, making a double 2 or 3 inch (5 cm or 7 cm) hem depending on the amount of fabric available. Mark the corner with a pin 'A'. (Fig. 46). Open the side hem. Open out one turn of the bottom hem. (Fig. 47). Make a diagonal fold of 45°, keeping pin on outer edge of the fold (Fig. 48). Fold 'C' inwards and 'B' inwards, pin and slip-stitch. (Fig. 49). When the lining is slip-stitched in place the result is a pleasing balanced corner. (Fig. 50.)

A Double Mitre.

A double mitre is used on the corners of an applied band. The band should be cut double the finished width plus hem allowance of ½ inch (1 cm) on each edge. Make a fold in line with the corner, machine at an angle of 45° from the centre of the fold as fig. 51. Trim away surplus fabric, leaving ¼ inch (½ cm) outside of the stitching. Press the seam open. Sew one edge of the band to the other fabric, right sides facing. Turn the band on to the back of the fabric and slip stitch the other edge into position, covering the first line of stitching. (Fig. 52.)

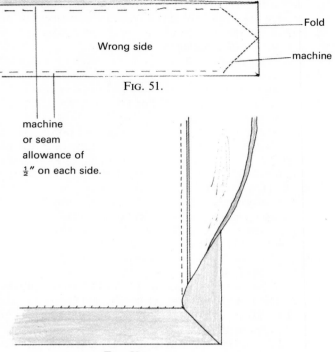

Fold

Wrong side

machine

FIG. 51.

machine
or seam
allowance of
$\frac{1}{2}''$ on each side.

FIG. 52.

CHAPTER THIRTEEN

Furnishing Fabrics

Brocade

Finely woven multi-coloured fabric, the design appearing on the face of the cloth being formed by extra weft threads. These extra threads appear on the back of the cloth in the form of stripes. Made from rayon, rayon and cotton, synthetic and combination of yarns. Used for bedcovers, cushion covers and curtains.

Brocatelle

Heavy, often rather stiff, figured fabric, with a pattern woven in relief. Brocatelle differs structurally from damask in that there is a non-essential weft thread, which is used to pad the figuring. Originally made in silk and linen, now often made of cotton and rayon, combined or individually. Probably originated from the Italian desire to imitate Venetian embossed leather work in a textile form. Used for upholstery and curtains.

Buckram

A coarse plain woven canvas, known as upholsterers buckram, stiffened with glue and size after weaving. Fabric can be adhered to the buckram by slightly damping the buckram and pressing the fabric on to it with a warm iron.

Bump and Domette

Both fabrics are woven from cotton waste.

Bump has a more fluffy surface and is also thicker than domette. Both are used as inter linings for bedcovers and curtains. Curtains interlined with bump have excellent insulation qualities, helping to keep out the window draughts and deadening sounds from the street.

Corduroy

From the French *Corde du Roi*, a strong cotton, possibly with a percentage of man-made yarns included. The fabric has a pile in the form of ribs running lengthwise, which vary from $\frac{1}{8}$ to 1 inch. The lighter weight is used for curtains and cushions; the heavier weight for upholstery.

Damask

A fabric of a single structure, i.e. one set only of warp and weft threads. The majority have satin weave backgrounds and the figuring in plain weave. In the 13th century the cloth was already known in England. The name is derived from Damascus. Damask is made in a variety of fibres including combinations of silk, linen, cotton and man-made mixtures. Used for curtains, bedcovers and loose-covers – (if for loose-covers, for those that will not be subjected to very hard wear).

Dralon

An acrylic fibre woven to make both flat and pile fabrics. Strong, it does not stain easily and is not attacked by insects. Used to make sheer curtains, draw curtains, and woven on to a cotton ground to make dralon velvet.

Dupion

A cloth that has a satin back and a slubby or textured front. Often of rayon, could be also woven in silk. Obtainable in a range of colours. Ideal for curtains but not suitable for loose-covers.

Calico

A strong cotton fabric, woven with a plain weave. Used as a base in a two-piece bed cover, and in upholstery beneath the final top cover.

Cambric (Downproofed)

A fine cotton fabric specially treated for the inner covers of eiderdowns and down cushions.

Casement cloth

An all-cotton fabric which used to be used as curtain lining; not so much used these days.

Chintz

A furnishing cloth of fine, closely woven cotton which

has a highly glazed surface and a stiff finish. Self coloured or printed with designs that are often traditional. This fabric is excellent as the outer covering of an eiderdown, as the glaze makes the fabric downproof, so eliminating the necessity of an inner downproof lining, thus making the eiderdown lighter in weight. It is also used for curtains, bedcovers and loose covers. Loose-covers, if made of chintz should be lined; this will help the cover to retain its shape and add strength.

Cretonne

Heavier than chintz, this cotton cloth is printed with various processes. Sometimes the warp is printed before weaving, thus giving the finished fabric a shadow effect, the cloth is then known as 'shadow tissue'. A strong cloth, used for curtains and loose-covers.

Felt

A non-woven fabric made from wool, difficult to wash. Easy to decorate with appliquéd embroidery. Used for cushions.

Fibre stitched fabric

This fabric is formed by fibres being held together by yarn which is chained stitched through the web of fibres forming a series of wales very close together running lengthwise through the fabric. This type of fabric drapes better than the adhesively bonded fabrics, which tend to be stiff. These fabrics are printed with a variety of designs. Used for curtains; not recommended for loose-covers.

Folkweave

A loosely woven fabric, using thickish yarns woven in a striped effect. As the name implies, it imitates the rough weave textures associated with village craft. Used for curtains, bedcovers and cushion covers.

Gingham

A fine, lightweight cotton of plain weave woven in checks. Ideal for unlined curtains, cushions and bed-covers.

Glass fabric

Spun from glass marbles – will not shrink, stretch or sag, is mothproof, fireproof and does not absorb dirt.

Glass fibre has low abrasion resistance, so should not be allowed to rub against rough sills or venetian blinds. If used as draw curtains, have a pull cord fitted to the curtain track to avoid pulling together by hand. Used for curtains only.

Linen and Linen-union

A strong fabric for furnishings, both plain and printed. When mixed with cotton but still with a predominance of linen it is known as linen-union, which is excellent for loose-covers. Used for curtains and loose-covers.

Matelasse

A double-cloth, one front and one back, with padding between. The fabric design is outlined by catching together the two layers, so holding the padding in position. Used mainly for upholstery; the lighter weight cloth for curtains.

P.V.C. (Polyvinyl Choride)

In thin plastic sheeting can be used for shower curtains. For the best results use metal eyelets on the curtain heading and hang with special pear-shaped rings from a rod. For upholstery it is a strong, sound, durable substitute for hides. Easily cleaned, wet resistant, comes in a variety of embossed effects. Also there are the expanded vinyl cloths, a soft P.V.C. laminated on to a thin foam base and supported by a knitted cotton back. This fabric can be obtained in a range of colours.

Repp

A plain weave fabric with a ribbed effect running across, caused by using alternate thick and thin threads, dyed in a range of colours. Used for curtains, bedcovers and loose-covers.

Satin

Furnishing material with a very smooth and lustrous finish; the weave is very close. Originally made in silk, but now produced in rayon, cotton and man-made fibres or a mixture of these fibres. The heavier weight is used for curtains, bedcovers and cushions; the lighter weight for eiderdowns.

Sateen

An all cotton fabric, used for curtain-linings. Dyed in a wide range of colours, but white or natural tend to be the most popular colour. This is because the strong light from the window tends to fade the coloured linings, causing unsightly streaks. Also used for lining of bedcovers.

Tapestry

Originally a hand-made woollen cloth, now made in cotton and worsted yarns. Some of the designs are an imitation of wool embroidery. A strong cloth, the heavier used for upholstery, the finer for curtains.

Taffeta

Plain weave self-coloured or shot-colour effect fabric, made in rayon and man-made fibres. This fabric is lightweight and has a sheen; mainly used for covering of eiderdowns; curtains and also cushions.

Terry cloth

Terry cloth or turkish towelling is a cotton fabric with a loose, loopy pile on both sides of the cloth. It can be purchased plain or printed in a range of colours and designs. It is ideal for bathroom curtains; the towelling will readily absorb the steam.

Terylene net curtaining

Terylene is a polyester fibre produced from petroleum. Net curtaining of today is very easy to care for in comparison to our Grandmothers day, when the heavy patterned cotton nets had to be starched and pulled carefully back to shape to hang correctly.

Velour

A rich pile fabric, comes in many grades. Made from cotton, cotton and rayon. Ideal for curtains and cushions.

CHAPTER FOURTEEN

Curtains and Pelmets

In the early 15th century, the buildings of the nobility had no windows as we know them. There were only narrow openings in the outer wall to let in a little light and air. The first curtain was probably the skin of an animal or a piece of coarse cloth hung to keep out the rain and cold.

In Tudor and Jacobean times, when glass came into use, windows became larger and curtains came into being. They were made to draw across the window on rings, hanging from a rod. The first curtains were single only; two curtains came later.

During the reign of Elizabeth I curtains were made of coloured silk or wool, often matching the bed draperies. Bay windows were a common feature of the Elizabethan manor. During the middle of the 17th and 18th centuries the walls were hung with expensive fabrics of brocade, damask and velvet, richly embroidered with gold and silver. The glass in the windows of those days consisted of small rectangular panes.

In early Elizabethan times the rod carrying the curtains was fixed at ceiling level, but when windows were fitted lower, a strip of cloth, the first valance, was used to hide the rod carrying the curtains. Later, there appeared the pelmet box, with a shaped top fixed over the rods and covered with cloth to match the curtains. Pelmets were elaborately trimmed and the curtains were held back during the day with silk cords, tassel-trimmed.

The drapery remained very ornate till after the reign of Victoria; from then to the present day draperies have

93

become very much lighter, and windows today are dressed to allow the entry of the maximum amount of light and air. Curtains are now draped back, often beyond the window opening itself, during the day. Though a period room may still call for elaborate drapery, this is more disciplined and less opulent than the draperies of the past.

To-days windows are often very large sheets of glass, providing much light and a view of the world outside. Curtains to furnish such large windows often cover an entire wall. The cost of buying the required yardage of cloth, with the necessary fullness widthwise to give the essential drape, demands that the curtains be used for as long as possible. With a little patience and ingenuity those curtains that are faded at the edges, too short, too narrow or need re-vitalising, can be made over and will give service and pleasure for a few more years.

Unlined curtains. If the curtains are too narrow or short or have faded front edges, the application of a contrasting border can be effective and attractive. This border should be of double fabric, i.e., wide enough to fold around onto the back, so giving a neat finish when viewed from either back or front. Choose a fabric for the additional border that will not fray too readily, is neither too thick, nor of too loose a weave.

If the curtain has previously been laundered, make sure the border will also be washable. Launder the new fabric before cutting to the size required, otherwise shrinkage will spoil the whole effect.

Applying the contrast border. Decide whether the border is to extend down the length of the curtain only, or across the lower edge of the curtain as well. When taking the border down the side edges and across the lower edge, a double mitre should be used. (Fig. 51 and 52.)

Remove the hooks, unpick the heading, wash or clean the curtains. If the curtains have faded on the front edges, cut away the faded sections. Decide on the width the border is to be, remembering that the material for the border must be cut double its finished width plus seam allowance; and lengthways, the border must be long enough to accommodate the making of a double mitre.

Sew border to the curtain as (Fig. 52).

Sew the heading tape to the top of the curtain, and slip in the required number of hooks. Press well.

On kitchen curtains of a plain fabric, the addition of a border of gingham with Ric-Rac edging outlining the seams of the border, will make an attractive practical decoration.

Fabric can be purchased with printed vertical bands of pattern, ideal for decorating curtains and bedcovers.

Fig. 53.

Lined curtains. Braids and ribbons of various widths are suitable border material. These can be set in a short distance away from the outer edge of the curtain, (Fig. 53). This is a practical solution where the curtains need to be extended in width and length by 1 ft (30 cm) or more.

Material for the decorative band, and also extra material for the plain border at the outer edges of the curtain, would be needed. Estimate for the required amount of fabric, remembering that a plain outer border will require more fabric than the inner band.

Applying a decorative and plain border to the side and bottom edge of a curtain. Unpick the edges of the curtain. If necessary, cut away any damaged or faded part. Make-up the outer and inner border and sew these together, then sew to the curtain.

The lining will require an extra strip widthwise and lengthwise to bring it to the larger size. Cut the width required, machine to present lining, and sew into place.

Ribbon decoration. Ribbon can be used effectively to enrich a curtain that is otherwise in good condition. Ribbon decoration needs careful planning and preparation. Plot out the design you have chosen onto pattern-making paper, the type used by dressmakers. To transfer this design to the curtain, first trace onto tissue paper by laying the tissue paper over the design and outlining with a pencil. Then pin the tissue paper carefully to the desired area along the side and lower edge of the curtain (having previously released the lining and pinned this back out of the way), with a contrasting colour cotton and, using small running stitches, outline the design. Tear the paper away and machine or hand sew the ribbon to the lines indicated. When the ribbon border is complete, resew the lining back into position.

FIG. 54.

Patchwork. Strip patchwork makes a practical and colourful border for lined curtains and bedcovers. (Fig. 54.)

Choose a fabric that will not fray too easily and is not too thick. Dress-weight cottons can be obtained in many designs and colours; if you make your own clothes you may have left-over pieces available.

For a richer effect, on more luxurious curtains, use light silks and satins.

Templates for patchwork are obtainable from haberdashery departments. Otherwise you can make your own from cardboard, making sure they are geometrically accurate. Cut exact paper shapes from the template; cartridge paper is good for this. Cut the fabric patchwork shapes plus $\frac{1}{4}$ inch (1 cm) on all edges. Tack stitch fabric over the paper shape (Fig. 55). When a number of fabric shapes have been tacked to the paper, oversew together, keeping them in the desired pattern. (Fig. 56.)

FIG. 55. Tack, stitching fabric over paper shape.

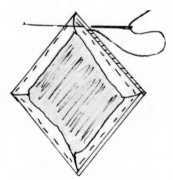

FIG. 56. Oversewing shapes together.

Adapting curtains of contrast design. A practical way to use 2 pairs of lined curtains of different designs or colour, is to cut and join them together in alternating strips. (See Fig. 57.) This is helpful if you want to

97

G

furnish a wider window or salvage the best pieces from faded or damaged curtains.

Unpick the curtains completely. Press flat and cut away any damaged areas. Decide how many vertical strips, and of what width, you will get out of each curtain front. Mark carefully with tailors chalk and cut (do not cut the linings). Seam alternate strips together, using a plain seam. Press all seams flat.

Fig. 57.

Press 1½ inches (4 cm) single turn on side edges of curtain. Press lower hem into position, allowing as much as possible for a double hem.

Mitre corners. (Figs. 46–49.) Serge sides, slip hem lower edge (Figs. 31 and 34). Join the curtain linings together. Reline the curtain.

Re-head, press and hang.

Fɪɢ. 58.

Lined and interlined curtains. Sometimes, after cleaning, lined and interlined curtains need adjustment because lining or front material has shrunk.

Unpick the edges holding the lining to the front fabric, including the heading. Lay the curtain flat on the floor and, keeping the lining a uniform distance up from the lower edge of the curtain, tack stitch it along.

Smooth both fabrics to the top of the curtain. If the seams are dragging where the lining and front fabric have been caught together, release these. Using a tape measure, metre or yard stick, measure the curtain length at intervals; turn the top edge of front and lining over together on to the back of the curtain and tack stitch.

Sew on the type of heading tape required.

Interlined curtains. The interlining of curtains often becomes disarranged during cleaning processes, especially if the interlining has not been properly sewn in at the edges during the making.

Again, undo all edges, unless the heading of the curtain is sewn in such a manner that you feel you could not resew it.

If all edges are unpicked, smooth fabrics towards the top of the curtain, if the heading is left intact, smooth fabric towards side and bottom edges. Lock stitch the interlining to the front fabric. (Fig. 59.) Sew the lower and side hems. (Fig. 60.)

Smooth the lining into position, tack stitch and then slip-stitch into place. Re-head if required.

Pelmets. Pelmets give windows a formal look; like the valance, they link and frame the window.

A pelmet consists of the face fabric, lining, and a stiffened interlining of upholsterers' buckram. This is a specially made canvas which has been stiffened with glue and size; it can be obtained in various weights and thicknesses. Always choose a good quality.

After some years of wear and dry-cleaning the buckram interlining tends to lose its stiffness, and crumble, but the front fabric may still be in good condition, so remaking is a worthwhile consideration.

Perhaps a new shaped lower edge will be required to give a fresh look to the window.

The depth of the pelmet is governed by the type of window being furnished, and, in the case of a remake,

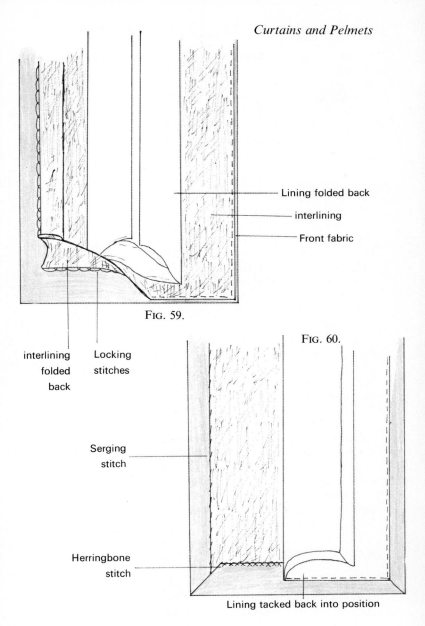

Lining folded back

interlining

Front fabric

FIG. 59.

interlining
folded
back

Locking
stitches

FIG. 60.

Serging
stitch

Herringbone
stitch

Lining tacked back into position

by the amount of fabric available. If the ceiling is low, avoid a pelmet that is too deep, as this will make the ceiling look lower still.

The shape of the pelmet will often be dictated by the fabric, if patterned. To team with vertically striped curtains, use the fabric horizontally for a pleasing effect on the pelmet; this may be possible if the furnishings are being adapted for a new window.

Remaking pelmets. Carefully unpick completely. Dry-clean or launder front fabric. Clean the trimming, if it is in a good condition, (test for colourfast before washing).

The lining may be stained, but try laundering before discarding it for new. If a new design for the lower edge is required, use some strong paper and make a template that will fit the window at the depth required. (Household articles, such as plates, can be used to draw curves). Continue to experiment till a satisfactory shape is obtained.

Measure the width and length of the template to calculate the amount of buckram required. Although buckram is usually made in the width of 36 inches (92 cm), some large furnishing stores will sell the buckram cut along the length; this avoids the necessity of joining. If joining is necessary, do not lap join, but butt together, reinforcing at the back with a strip of buckram 1 inch ($2\frac{1}{2}$ cm) wide; use copy-dex or sew by hand.

Cut the new shape from the paper template or from the old buckram. Do not at any stage attempt to fold the buckram, always roll it. If the buckram becomes cracked, it is impossible to remove the deep indent; this crack would always be discernible in the finished article.

A thin front fabric will require an interlining over the buckram face, to prevent the coarse texture of the buckram from showing through.

Interlining can be a domette, bump or even an old flannelette sheet.

Using $\frac{1}{2}$ inch ($1\frac{1}{2}$ cm) tacking stitches, tack the interlining $\frac{1}{4}$ inch ($\frac{1}{2}$ cm) in from the edge of the buckram. (Diagram 61.) Trim the interlining so that it is level with the edge of the buckram. Lay buckram, covered with

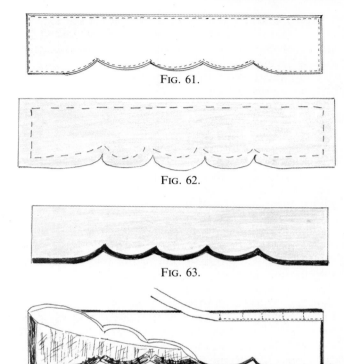

Fig. 61.

Fig. 62.

Fig. 63.

Fig. 64.

interlining, right side uppermost. Place the top fabric in place over the interlining, making sure that at least $\frac{3}{4}$–1 inch (2–3 cm) of the top fabric overlaps the buckram all around. (Diagram 62.)

Using long tacking stitches, secure to buckram. (Diagram 62.) Clip lower edge at concave shapings. Turn pelmet over, face downwards.

Slightly damp the outer edge of the buckram and press the fabric in place with a warm iron.

Apply trimming, using either adhesive or hand sewing. (Fig. 63). Sew the lining to the pelmet, leaving a margin of $\frac{1}{4}$ inch ($\frac{1}{2}$ cm) all round the edge.

103

Apply a tacking tape (diagram 64) by sewing a strong tape about 1 inch (2½ cm) wide near the top of the pelmet; being sure to catch the buckram without penetrating through to the right side.

Leave the top edge of the tape loose, making a line of stitches across the tape at 4 inch (10 cm) intervals, so forming the pockets, through which the tacks will go when fixing the pelmet in place.

Net curtains (Fine weave). Most of todays nets are made of man-made fibres or mixed with natural ones; shrinkage is not a great problem. But if you are moving house, you may wish to adjust the curtains to fit a window of a different size. Widthwise the nets can be joined together without much trouble; but lengthwise, additions need more thinking about.

Four suggestions illustrated are :–

The addition of a gathered frill to the lower edge. (Fig. 65). Cut the frill so that, if possible, it has twice the amount of fabric widthways as the curtain. The depth of the frill should be cut 2 inches (5 cm) deeper than the required finished size. Join the strips into one long piece. Make a narrow hem each end and a narrow lower hem. Turn the top edge to form a double ½ inch (1½ cm) hem. Gather this hem on the stitch line ½ inch (1½ cm) down. Right sides uppermost, sew frill to the lower edge of the curtain at the gathering of the frill. (Fig. 66.)

Lace insertion can be very attractive and practical. Cut the curtain through at the desired level and turn the raw edges of the two curtain pieces over ¼ inch (1 cm) and press onto the right side. Lay lace to cover these small turnings, tack stitch and machine twice (Fig. 67) or zig-zag.

Pleated lower edge. Unpick lower edge and press out hem, cut pleated section twice the depth required plus hem allowance, 4½ inches (11 cm). Join pleated section to main curtain, make a series of pleats. Finish the lower hem with a double 2 inch (5 cm) hem. (Fig. 68.)

False heading. Unpick the heading of the curtain. This will make the curtain 3 or 4 inches (7½ or 10 cm) longer.

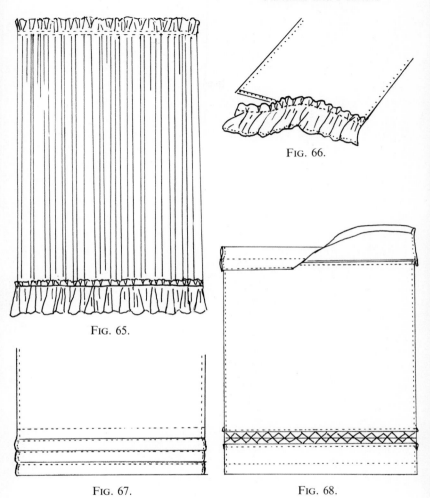

Fig. 66.

Fig. 65.

Fig. 67.

Fig. 68.

Cut a strip of net to the required depth and stitch to the head as diagram. (Fig. 67.)

CHAPTER FIFTEEN

Curtain Tracks, Tapes and Trimmings

Curtain tracks. Adapting curtains for the furnishing of another window may mean the purchasing of a new suspension rail.

Todays curtain tracks are unobtrusive, streamlined and easy to manage. The modern tracks do not require a pelmet and reveal as little as possible of the working mechanics. They are made from a variety of materials; extruded plastic, aluminium or brass rails, with nylon fittings, glides and attachments.

They can be face-fixed or top-fixed, and incorporate a cording set if required; some may have an overlap system to ensure that the curtains come together adequately when pulled across the window.

FIG. 69. Neta rail.

Some tracks have hook-runners combined, thus making the curtain hook unnecessary, the curtains being attached to the rail by hooking into the pocketed heading tape.

The rails can be concealed when the curtains are drawn by a stand-up heading.

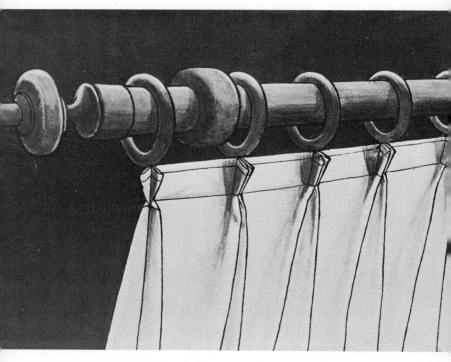

<small>Fig. 70. Wooden pole and rings.</small>

Victorian and Edwardian brass or wooden poles are popular. (Diagram 70.) These are elegant plain or reeded brass poles with decorative ends, or white enamelled poles with rounded ball ends and wooden or brass rings. Plain whitewood poles can be painted to match wall paper or curtains. Brass poles can also be purchased to adjust telescopically to the window width.

If a pelmet is required always fix a lathe, that is a

wooden shelf held by brackets, above the window head, the curtain track being fixed to the underside of the lathe.

Before making a final choice of a curtain rail, visit furnishing departments, collect leaflets and inspect the range available.

Fix the curtain track of your choice above and beyond the window frame if possible; this will allow the curtains to hang on the wall when drawn back, so giving maximum daylight.

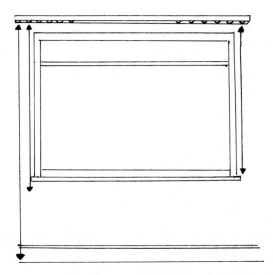

FIG. 71. Three recommended curtain lengths.

Recommended curtain lengths are:– a) To the sill. b) 3 or 4 inches (8 to 10 cm) below the sill. c) Just to clear the carpet. (Fig. 71.)

Curtain Heading Tapes. There are a variety of heading tapes avaiable for the home curtain maker; these give a choice of pleats or gathers.

Your decision will depend on the amount of fabric widthwise in your curtains. For triple pleats, using the 'Deep pleat' tape, the material width required is $2\frac{1}{2}$

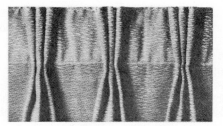

FIG. 72. Deep pleats.

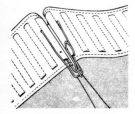  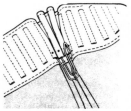

SINGLE PLEATS   DOUBLE PLEATS   TRIPLE PLEATS

Make sure pocket openings are at lower edge of tape. Stitch on tape flush with top edge of curtain, neatening ends.

FIG. 73. Single, double and triple pleats.

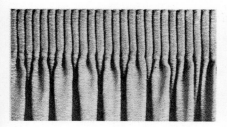 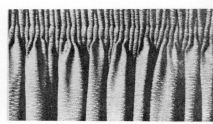

FIG. 74. Pencil pleats.   FIG. 75. Standard Rufflette tape.

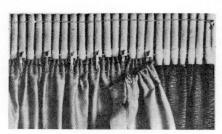

110

FIG. 76. Lining tape.

times the curtain track. (Figs. 72 and 73.) For luxurious pencil pleats using 'Regis' tape, again $2\frac{1}{2}$ times the curtain track width is recommended. (Fig. 74.) If the curtains have only a little fullness widthways, use a Standard pleating tape. (Fig. 75.)

Perhaps after renovating your curtains you may wish to make the cleaning of lined curtains easier. In this case, make the front and lining as two separate items and use lining tape on the curtain lining. This will enable the lining to be attached to the curtain by the same hooks which suspend the curtain from the track. (Fig. 76.)

Trimmings. In early times trimmings such as braids, fringes, and tassels were used to decorate harnesses, and these were adapted to interior decoration during the 14th century.

Many of the early trimmings came from Italy. The English craftsmen copied these imports and became skilled trimming makers. From the early 18th century to Victorian times curtains were heavily decorated with deep fringes and cords. To-day, trimmings are used with restraint.

The term 'trimming' applied to furnishing includes fringes, braids, cord and tassels. Gimps are used mainly on upholstery.

The choice of a trimming must be in keeping with its fitness for the purpose. Keep the weight of the trimming in unison with the fabric. An expensive fabric must have an accompanying trimming of the same class. See that the heading has a firm finish, and the yarns used on the skirt are even.

Types of trimming.

Ball – small balls of cotton, silk, or rayon forming the skirt.

Bouclé – a fringe with a skirt of twisted yarn.

Cluster – a fringe in which the skirt has a graded edge with points like the edge of a saw.

Boullion – a fringe with a skirt of twisted loops, ranging from medium to very thick.

Twine fringe – a very fine boullion.

Gimp – used mainly in upholstery. This is a narrow

111

braid and has a loose weave of thread-warped cords forming a pattern. (Tacks may be hidden under this decoration).

Gallons or galons – narrow ribbon-like braid with bright decoration; metal threads are sometimes used.

Ruches – narrow woven trimming, used on cushions and loose covers and upholstery when rich fabrics such as brocades, damask, velour and velvet are used. There are two types of ruches; the pile of the trimming is attached to a centre core, and the loops which form the decoration can be either cut or uncut.

Tassel – a fringe with a heading and a skirt of evenly spaced tassels.

Knotted – skirt cords crossed and knotted together, also trimmed with tassels.

Moulded or pendant – small pendant 'drops' of wood covered in silky yarn. These are more suitable for lamp-shades than soft furnishing.

The purpose of trimmings. When used on a pelmet, trimmings emphasize the shaped edge, drawing attention to the draperies and defining them from their surroundings. On curtains they define a contrast border or hide a seam when the curtains have been adapted to make them wider. On bedcovers they decorate and hide seams. Used on furniture, trimmings conceal the method of attaching the upholstered cover. Loose-covers, cut so that the lower edge finishes level with the upholstery, are often trimmed around the lower edge with a deep bullion fringe. This adds weight to the lower edge of the cover so that it hangs better, and also adds a decorative touch. Lamp-shades are trimmed with a braid or fringe of appropriate weight, so hiding and neatening the edges and adding decorative appeal. Rugs, too, are sometimes trimmed with a heavy fringe.

The range of colours in trimming is extensive; choose a trimming by daylight, matching it with a sample of the fabric it will enrich. Hand sew the trimmings on to curtains, bed covers or pelmets, unless you are sure that if you machine them in place you can keep a perfectly straight line; any deviation will be very obvious. Ruches can be machined to cushions provided they are tacked-stitched into position first.

H

CHAPTER SIXTEEN

Bedcovers

In the Middle Ages beds were treasured pieces of furniture. In the families of the nobility, and rich merchants, the best bed was handed down to the heirs. The draperies were luxurious and very costly, made of velvet, silk or damask and often encrusted with magnificent embroidery and silver and gold threads. These beds could cost anything from between £1500 and £3000, which was a tremendous sum in those days.

The medieval bed of the nobleman consisted of a pair of 'bed stocks', a wooden structure of four rails joined to four short posts for the legs. Holes were bored in the rails and strong cord threaded through to form a base for the mattress. The mattress was of plaited rushes. On top of this would lie a feather bed. Feather pillows and bolsters were also used. The draperies were the dominant feature; they consisted of a 'tester' and curtains. The tester was a canopy over the head of the bed, suspended from the ceiling. Sometimes the canopies were shaped like tents and called 'sparvers'. The curtains were hung from rings and, when drawn, completely enclosed the bed. The bed was warm, comfortable and draughtproof, in surroundings that were cold and often uncomfortable; the manors and castles had stone walls and ceilings, and though the walls were hung with valuable tapestry, these rooms often had inadequate heating.

It is small wonder that the owners of such beds were

loath to leave them; so they entertained their friends, and ate, besides sleeping, in their beds. The ordinary man had a much less spectacular and costly bed, the bed drapery being usually of linen cloth, printed with a design imitating a tapestry, the walls hung with matching fabric. The mattress of the bed would usually be of wool or flock, though servants or the very poor slept on straw mattresses.

The first four-poster beds appeared in England in the 15th century and began to supersede the suspended canopy. In the 16th century the woodwork of the beds was elaborate and carved, but the rich still favoured the draped bed with rich fabrics covering the woodwork.

In 1672 a French upholsterer made the court a richly draped four-poster, with 'window' curtains and chairs and stools in matching damask. This introduced upholstered bedroom furniture.

In the early 19th century the Regency style appeared. The woodwork and draperies of the bed became lighter. The embroidered motifs of these draperies, which had previously been of heavy tree patterns, now gave way to sprays of flowers.

The rooms of this time were smaller than before and better heating was possible; so the need for the curtains enclosing the bed disappeared and only those at the bed head remained.

Victorian times bought the iron and brass bed which is still with us, though in a lighter form than the original.

To-days bedrooms can be smooth and silky, fussy, or simple. The furnishings may be traditional or contemporary according to the personal taste of the occupant. They may be used only for sleeping, or as private retreats, somewhere to think, read, work or entertain.

Whether it is a single or dual purpose room, the main piece of furniture is naturally the bed, Maximum comfort should be the aim; there are beds to suit all tastes.

A worn bed that sags in the middle is bad for the occupant or occupants, giving no support for the spinal muscles; similarly too soft a bed can fail to give the necessary support. Too hard a bed will not cradle the body hollows behind the waist and knee.

Width and length are most important. The bed should be big enough widthways to allow you to clasp your arms behind your head without your elbows overhanging the sides. For adequate length the bed should be 6 inches (15 cm) longer than your height.

Recommended metric bed sizes (and equivalent Imperial measurements).

Double bed

Standard	150×200 cm	$(4'-11'' \times 6'-6\frac{3}{4}'')$.
Double bed Small	135×192 cm	$(4'-5'' \times 6'-3\frac{1}{2}'')$.
Single standard	100×200 cm	$(3'-3\frac{3}{8}'' \times 6'-6\frac{3}{4}'')$.
Small	85×192 cm	$(2'-9\frac{1}{2}'' \times 6'-3\frac{1}{2}'')$.

People sharing a bed sometimes prefer different types of mattresses; to suit them a mattress can be acquired which is really two, connected together by a strong snap fastening. If a bed is difficult to move, castors should be fitted. Twin beds are easy to move and make but bunk beds, although space savers, are difficult to make up.

The bed base is usually one of two kinds;

Sprung edge, meaning that the springs are continued to the very edge of the bed, and stand up above the wooden frame, making the edge soft.

Firm edge divans with a wooden frame making the edge of the bed hard. The sprung edge is the most expensive of the two.

For the bedroom furnished in the grand manner the romance of the fourposter is not a thing of the past, but obtainable in a lighter form with wood or metal frames and easy care Terylene draperies.

Bed heads are made in various designs and materials i.e., cane, wood, lacquered metal, brass or buttoned upholstery.

Pillows may be filled with feather and down, terylene or foam. Two kinds of foams are used for bed pillows, latex and polyther. Latex foam is made from liquid rubber. It is strong and resilient, germ repellant and non-allergenic. Pillows of latex can be carefully washed by hand. Polyther foam is made from a mixture of chemicals; the density can be chemically controlled,

117

making it either hard or soft.

Always store a foam pillow in an extra pillow-slip as the filling can be damaged by exposure to the light.

Various types of beds need various types of bedcover.

Repair and renovation of the following styles will be considered:

Throw-over.

Fitted one-piece.

Fitted two-piece.

Feather quilts (eiderdown and duvets).

Wadded quilts.

Throw-over bedcovers. These are the simplest bed-covers, consisting of flat rectangular pieces of cloth. The two lower ends may be cut in a rounded shape to lessen the danger of catching the feet on the trailing ends. (Fig. 77A.)

To obtain the correct cutting line for the rounded ends, place the cover on the bed, over the blankets that would be in normal use, and mark each corner with pins. Cut below this line, allowing at least 1 inch ($2\frac{1}{2}$ cm), or more if required, for seam allowance. (Fig. 77B.)

The materials suitable for throw-over bedcovers are a variety of soft furnishing fabrics, i.e. prints, dupions,

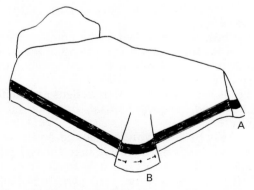

FIG. 77. Throw-over bedcover, with pins in place.

tweeds, damask and many various weaves and fibres, with a little caution in choice where a very loose weave is concerned; this can catch on rings and buttons which damages the fabric structure.

The amount of fabric required for an average double bed throw-over is 6 yards (6 metres) of 48″ or 50″ wide material. This would make a bedcover of approximately 7 ft 8 inches (234 cm) to 7 ft 10 inches (240 cm) wide by 8 ft 9 inches (270 cm) long.

Perhaps your present throw-over bedcover is in a good condition, but too short in width and length. You can remedy this by:

Inserting a contrast band about 4 inches (10 cm) in from the edge of the bedcover. (Fig. 78.)

Adding a contrast border. (Fig. 79.)

Trimming with a deep buillion fringe.

When joining pieces of the same fabric together, to bring the bedcover to the width desired, decorate these seams with piping, or camouflage with braid.

Perhaps you have two single bedcovers of different

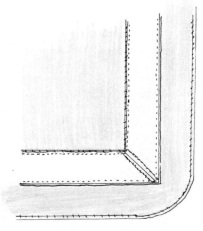

FIG. 78. Contrast band.

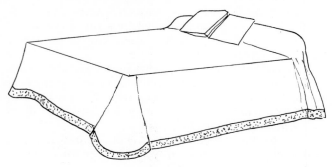

FIG. 79. Contrast border.

designs and texture that could be combined in a pleasing patchwork manner; or a double-size throw-over that could be allied with fabric from an unwanted pair of curtains still in a good condition. Why not use them to make a simple patchwork throw-over? The construction of the patchwork is very simple and can be sewn together by machine.

A double size bedcover in patchwork, using large squares; finished size of each, 8 inches (20 cm). The patchwork illustrated will measure, when finished, 8 ft (244 cm) wide by 8 ft 8 inches (262 cm) long.

Adjust this width and length, if necessary, either by adding extra squares or by making the existing ones larger.

The bedcover will require 156 squares. These must be cut to the following sizes:

2 of each colour	$10\frac{1}{2} \times 10\frac{1}{2}$ inches $(27 \times 27$ cm)	(one for each corner)
21 of each colour	$9 \times 10\frac{1}{2}$ inches $(23 \times 27$ cm)	(the squares for the outer edges)
55 of each colour	9×9 inches $(23 \times 23$ cm)	(the inner squares)

156 squares in all.

This bedcover should be lined, to cover the many seams on the wrong side.

Join any existing lining to the required width and

length. If purchasing new lining material, buy a sateen curtain lining in a toning colour, 6 yards (6 metres) of 48 inch (127 cm) width. Cut the lining into two 3 yards (3 metre) lengths and then cut one piece through lengthwise down the centre fold.

You now have one full width and two half widths.

Join the half width to either side of the full width by machining at $\frac{1}{2}$ inch ($1\frac{1}{2}$ cm) in from the edge, making a flat seam.

Press open both seams. Fold carefully and lay aside till required.

Taking care to place patches in their correct sequence, the larger on the outer edges, and taking $\frac{1}{2}$ inch ($1\frac{1}{2}$ cm) seam allowance on all edges, join together, making individual cross strips. Press open seams. Join these cross strips together to make the whole. Press open seams.

Shape the lower ends if required, leaving 2 inches (5 cm) beyond the shaping for seam allowance. Turn the edges in for 2 inches (5 cm) and press.

Mitre back corners, (and front corners if unshaped). Catch the single hem back using a serging or herringbone stitch. (Fig. 30 or 31.) Ease the fullness evenly on the inner edge of the curved hem.

Press the edges of the bedcover.

Spread the bedcover out on table or floor, wrong side uppermost. Lay the lining on top, right side uppermost. Fold back the lining and make three rows of locking stitches vertically, catching bedcover and lining together.

Smooth lining back in place and turn edges under, leaving a $1\frac{1}{2}$ inches (4 cm) margin of bedcover all around. Tack stitch in place and slip stitch.

Press well.

If a throwover bedcover that is otherwise in a good condition has acquired a stain or a burn, cover the impaired section with appliquéd shapes; bands of contrast fabric; machine embroidery; hand embroidery or crochet bands and panels.

Tailored or fitted bedcovers. Fitted bedcovers take

more fabric than throw-overs, but give the bed an air of luxury and distinction.

The rise of the pillows must be taken into consideration. A pillow-flap, which is an oblong additional part sewn to the top of the bedcover, is one of the most satisfactory ways of covering the pillows.

The bed is made up in the usual manner, except for the pillows; these are placed in position after the bedcover is in place and the flap is then brought up and turned down over the pillows. (Fig. 80.)

Instead of the pillows-flap, a wedge shape can be inserted each side, between the bed-top and skirt, or valance, at the bed-head. This method is satisfactory providing the gussets are cut to the height and length of the pillows. If the gusset is too large it will give a loose untidy look instead of a neat, tailored appearance; if too

FIG. 80. Bedcover with pillow-flap.

small it will cause the bedcover to lift at the head, making the floor line uneven. (Fig. 81.)

The bedcover with a graduated frill which accommodates the rise of the pillow is most convenient for bed making. This type of frill has greater depth at the head of the bed.

Separate day-covers for pillows give a bed a well-dressed appearance, but some people find the necessity of transferring the pillows to their cases, and vice versa, on rising and retiring, a tedious chore. (Fig. 82.)

A tailored bedcover may also be made in two pieces, the valance being treated as one separate item, the bed-top being the other. If this method is used the valance remains permanently in position.

Fitted Bedcovers. The two fitted bedcovers (Fig. 81 and 82 could be made from two throwovers or from curtains of different design, so long as the fabric was in a good condition.

Unpick the bedcovers or curtains. Launder or dry-clean.

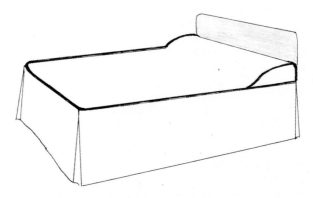

FIG. 81. Tailored bedcover.

Measure the length and the width of the bed, over the bedclothes. Measure the height of the bed, with the bedclothes in position.

Spread the cloth flat on a large surface. Chalk out the

FIG. 82. Separate day covers for pillows.

required components, plus hem allowance.

The skirt can be finished in various ways according to the weight and nature and amount of cloth available, i.e. kick-pleats, gathered flounce, or just a plain skirt. The bedcover may be lined or unlined.

The pillow cases should finish about an inch (2 cm) larger in width and length than the pillows, the opening being a 'house-wife' flap.

Seam together the bed-top if necessary. Seam the widths of the skirt together. Make a narrow hem along the bottom edge of the shirt. Gather or pleat the top edge of the skirt to fit the bed-top.

Trim with piping around the two sides and bottom edges of the bed-top.

Sew the skirt to the bed-top and press well.

Two-piece bedcover with separate valance and bed-top. This is the type of bedcover where the valance remains in position, keeping hidden the space under the bed and the bed legs. (Fig. 83). The valance can be gathered, box-pleated or plain with inverted pleats at the lower corners.

The base consists of a calico platform cut the same size as the box spring, plus turnings. The valance is sewn to this along the two sides and at the foot.

The mattress is placed on the top and the bed made up in the usual manner; the separate bed-top covering the bed clothes.

The bedcover top can either be a shortened version of a throw-over or be tailored. For the throw-over bedcover that has become torn or shabby around the edge, reduce the length and the width of the bed-cover, so that when finally adjusted, with the blankets in position, it will fall 2 to 3 inches (5 to $7\frac{1}{2}$ cm) below the mattress level.

Making an independent bed-base. The measurements to be taken, including seam allowances, are as follows:–

Length and width of box spring, plus $\frac{1}{2}$ inch ($1\frac{1}{2}$ cm) allowance at sides and foot and 2 inches (5 cm) at the head end.

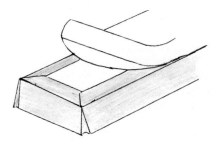

FIG. 83.

Height from the box-spring to the floor plus 2 inches (5 cm) for hems and seam allowance.

First cut the platform in calico, or some other strong fabric, allowing for joining if the fabric is not wide enough.

Cut the facing for the platform. This is necessary because, when the bed is in use, the blankets tucked under the mattress cause it to rise and there is a tendency for the edges of the base to be seen.

Cut the valance allowing for the style required, i.e.

Gathered (Fig. 86).

Box-pleated (Figs. 104 and 105).

125

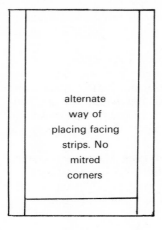

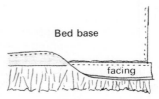

Bed base

facing

FIG. 84.   FIG. 85.

Kick-pleats on corners (Fig. 83).

Seam together the calico base, if necessary. Make a double 1 inch (2 cm) seam across the back edge.

Join together the widths for the valance. Make a double ¾ inch (2 cm) hem at the bottom and sides, mitring the corners; gather, pleat or leave plain the top edge. Make to fit the platform. (Fig. 86.)

If a lined valance is needed proceed as (Figs. 101 to 103 Loose cover section), then pleat or gather the top edge.

Join together the strips for the facing of the platform edge. (Figs. 84 or 86.) Machine the valance to the platform as (Fig. 85). Machine the facing to the platform as (Fig. 85). Machine the inner edge of the facing into place; Sew on tapes to tie to bed strutts at the head of the bed, and press well.

Feather and down quilts (Traditional). Bed quilts with down or a mixture of feather and down are often referred to as eiderdowns. This is technically incorrect. The down from the eider duck is very difficult to obtain and consequently very expensive.

Most of the fillings now being used are either down, which is the undercoating of water fowl, duck, goose or

126

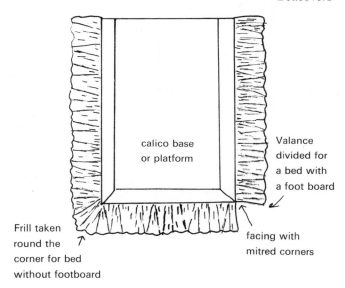

calico base
or platform

Valance
divided for
a bed with
a foot board

Frill taken
round the
corner for bed
without footboard

facing with
mitred corners

swan, consisting of the light fluffy material but without
the quill shaft. Owing to the natural difficulties of
complete separation, the inclusion of up to 15% by
weight, of fine, small, light, fluffy feathers is usually
permissable. Very resilient, buoyant, and the best
insulator in relation to weight, down is durable but
expensive.

A mixture of feather and down, where the feather
content is predominant in the mixture. (Ordinary
feathers, or soft milled feathers, are not suitable, as the
sharp stalks soon penetrate the top coverings.)

Choose the best quality possible when filling a quilt
or adding extra to a renovation. Weight is an important
feature, and the finer the quality of filling the lighter the
weight of the finished quilt. Not only will the better
filling provide a lightweight bed covering, it will also
give a warmer one. The filling traps air and so insulates
the sleeper, keeping the warmth in and the cold out.

Fabrics used as covers for quilts must also be as

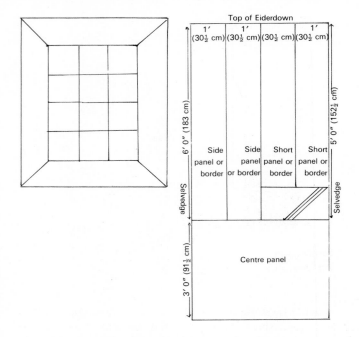

FIG. 87. A simple shape for the stitching that will form pockets for the filling.

FIG. 88. Cutting plan for an average double eiderdown, using 48″ fabric.

lightweight as possible. They may include silk, crepe, taffeta, satin, printed cambrics, poult, morocain and chintz. Of these, only cambrics and chintz are down-proof. The other fabrics will need a down-proof inter-lining of waxed cambric.

The underside of a quilt is usually of a down-proof cambric or down-proof sateen, chosen to tone with the top cover. It is unwise to cover both sides with silky fabrics as the slightest movement of the sleeper will then send the quilt sliding to the floor.

The quilt will be stitched through all its thickness, forming panels; not only is this decorative, but it holds and defines the even distribution of the down. (Figs. 87–88.)

During continued use the front cover can become stained and shabby, while the back may be in a good condition, or maybe only the corners are worn. The eiderdown illustrated (Fig. 90) has a worn area on the back outer corner, the rest of the back cover is in a good condition. The front is also in a reasonable state, but a new front cover will give fresh visual appeal, as well as a new lease of life, to a still useful article.

Before part recovering, or carrying out any repairs, have the quilt dry-cleaned, either by a reliable establishment or do-it-yourself cleaners. Be sure to air the quilt well in the open air after using a coin-operated dry-cleaning unit.

Measure the width and length of the eiderdown and calculate the amount of fabric required. Take an accurate template or measurements of stitched channels or panels holding the down in position. (Fig. 89.)

To hide and repair the damaged underside corner, the new top cover will extend over and onto the back.

Cut new fabric as plan. (Fig. 88.)

Cut away the top cover, without damaging the under downproof cover. Trim away frilled edging or piping cord, again taking care not to cut the downproof interlining. (Fig. 91.)

If the former cover is of chintz, downproof sateen or cambric, there may be no downproofed interlining. If this is so, carefully remove edge trim, i.e. piping or frilling, only.

If the eiderdown seems a little flat, unpick the outer edge seam for about 6 inches and add some more filling. Carefully oversew gap.

If some of the added down is required to give the centre panels a lift, unpick small gateways of stitching leading into these panels and slap the eiderdown with the flat of the hand, so forcing the extra down through. Be sure to close these openings again with small back

129

J

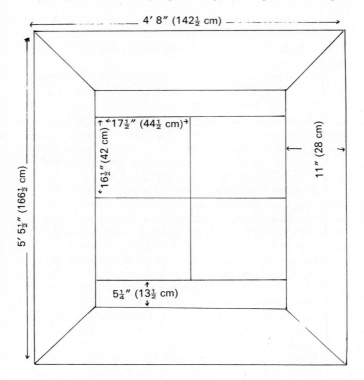

FIG. 89. Finished size of eiderdown.

stitches. Join front and back borders in their correct sequence, making mitred seams. Press open seams.

Using a contrast cotton and small tacking stitches, mark the new centre panel by outlining the design used to hold the down in place. Any decoration required, such as contrast bands of ribbon etc., should be sewn to new centre panel.

Machine the borders to the centre panel. Pipe the outer edge, or add a narrow frill if required. Machine the back borders to the front borders.

130

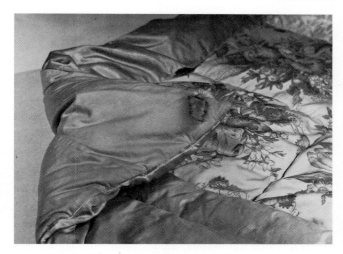

Fig. 90. Damaged underside corner.

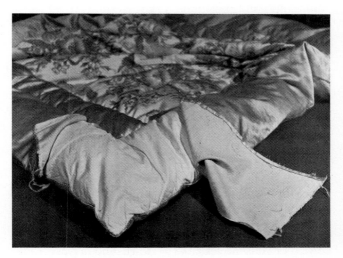

Fig. 91. Cutting away the top cover.

Lay the eiderdown on to a large working surface, spread out flat.

Lay the new top cover in position on top, back-stitch the centre panel to the eiderdown, following the stitching holding the down.

Fold back the front border and, using locking stitches of about $1\frac{1}{2}$ inches long, secure the outer edges together.

Turn the eiderdown over and slip-stitch the outer edge of the back border to the back of the eiderdown. (Fig. 6). Shake well. For finished eiderdown see Fig. 92.

Duvets or Continental Quilts. Maybe you have an old eiderdown that you no longer wish to use, but the filling is of a good quality. Why not use the filling from the eiderdown and, with the addition of a little extra purchased filling, make a duvet bedcover, thus transforming an unwanted article into something useful?

Continental quilts (alias, duvet, dune, dunna, downie, or dyne), have become popular over the last few years and now tend to vie with the traditional blankets and eiderdown as bed furnishings. They eliminate blanket fluff and, with a fitted undersheet, they only require smoothing into position. Their warmth is equal to approximately three blankets and an eiderdown.

When buying filling for a duvet, choose the best you can afford.

Duck feather and down; contains approximately 20% down mixed with fine feathers.

Duck down and feather; not to be confused with the feather and down mixture, consists of 51% pure down blended with a lesser proportion of small curly feathers. This mixture makes a very light traditional duvet. The filling has good durability because of the springy texture of the feathers. The filling expands and traps air, so forming insulation. Down and feather will give the luxury of a traditional duvet without the expense of an all down filling.

Duck down; Pure duck down is not possible as one could never separate all the feathers completely; duck down contains at least 85% down and a very small proportion of fine feathers. In terms of lightness, duck

F<small>IG</small>. 92. New top cover, showing back border or lining that will hide the damaged underside.

down is only bettered by goose or eiderdown. In terms of comfort and softness pure duck down is only bettered by goose or eiderdown and will last a life time and be well worth the extra expense.

Goosedown; White goose down clusters are the dearest, most efficient insulators obtainable for duvets, with the possible exception of eiderdown which could cost as much as £150 for a single duvet and £275 for a double size.

Goose down is collected from Siberia, Canada and the Arctic.

A continental quilt should be long enough to cover the feet and shoulders with ease, and 18 inches (46 cm) wider than the bed. They can also be tailored to fit individual requirements.

The approximate sizes are:–

Small single for a 3 ft bed (92 cm), 4 ft 6 inches (137 cm) wide × 6 ft 6 inches (198 cm) long.

Small double.

For a 4 ft to a 4ft 6 inch bed, 6 ft (183 cm) wide ×
6 ft 6 inches (198 cm) long.

Standard double.

For a 5 ft wide bed, 6 ft 6 inches (198 cm) × 6 ft
6 inches (198 cm) long.

The filling is loose within a bag, or separated by
vertical inner fabric walls, so that the filling does not
vary in depth, but provides all-over insulation, unlike
eiderdowns in which the channels are stitched flat
through the fabric so reducing the insulating properties.
(Fig. 93.)

Down and feather proof cambric. The down and
feather or down filling must be contained in a good
down proof cambric case. This should be of a very good
quality, because the cheap grade of feather proof fabrics
will not prevent the fine feather filaments from penetrating through, so causing much annoyance and waste.
Feather proof cambric is 54 or 60 inches wide (137 cm
to $152\frac{1}{2}$ cm).

Making-up the inner case for a duvet. Buy the amount
of downproof cambric required (see Figs. 94 & 96).

Cut as plan (Fig. 94 & 96). When joining widths
together for the top or bottom of the cover use a double
stitched lapped seam (Fig. 97).

Make vertical walls. Apply as for the walls in a
sectioned inner cushion, (see page 146), the only differences being that the cushion cover has the walls running
across instead of downwards, and whereas the cushion
walls are slightly shaped, the duvet walls are straight.

Construct in the same manner as the cushion, complete with outside stitching. Take the old eiderdown and
unpick the stitching that is holding the down in the
defined spaces. Try not to cut or tear the cover. If this
happens, immediately sew together again to prevent the
seepage of feathers. When all the retaining channels have
been released, shake the feathers down to one corner and
machine across, so keeping the feathers in one area.

Unpick an edge seam in this section for about 12
inches (30 cm), and sew by hand to the open end of one

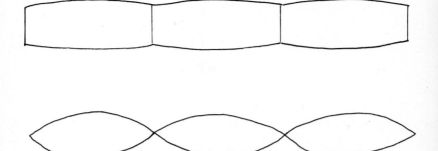

FIG. 93. Correct construction of duvet, above, contrasted with eiderdown, below.

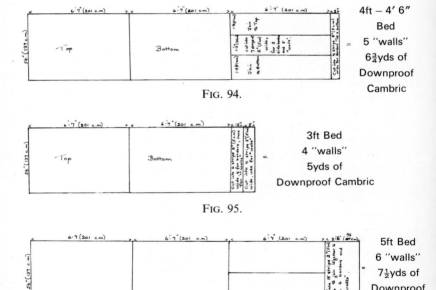

FIG. 94.

4ft – 4' 6"
Bed
5 "walls"
6¾yds of
Downproof
Cambric

FIG. 95.

3ft Bed
4 "walls"
5yds of
Downproof Cambric

FIG. 96.

5ft Bed
6 "walls"
7½yds of
Downproof
Cambric

135

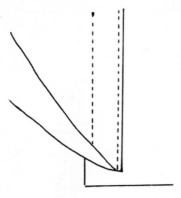

FIG. 97.

of the channels in the duvet. Beat with the hands on the feathers in the eiderdown. This will cause the feathers to travel into the duvet. When a satisfactory amount of feathers has passed through, carefully unpick the eiderdown from the duvet. Finely sew the duvet channel together and repeat with the other channels.

An amount of purchased down and feather will be required to complete the duvet.

Duvet outercovers can be purchased ready made, or you can make your own in Terylene and cotton fabric. These loose-covers are virtually a large bag, with an opening along one edge large enough to enable them to be slipped on to the duvet easily, the opening being closed by zip, velcro or tie-tapes.

Wadded Quilts. The popular wadded quilt, easy to care for and wash, is ideal as a bedcover for young children.

When a toddler grows and must leave the drop-side cot for a small single bed, the cot quilt may still be in a good condition and worth enlarging for use on the single bed. This can be done by adding a padded tube to all four sides. The filling will be encased in a fold of fabric with a double mitre on each corner. (Figs. 51 & 52.)

Calculate the amount of top covering that will be

136

needed to make the four tubes, remembering that if the
finished tube is to be 6 inches wide (15 cm), the fabric
width of the tube will be:– Double 6 inches + 1 inch for
seam allowance + 2 inches for the take-up of the padding
= 15 inches (38 cm).

Measure the side of the eiderdown, and across the
eiderdown. Usually the length is greater than the width.
To this length add the length of the width of the border
i.e. 15 inches (38 cm).

The choice of fabric should be of the same class as the
quilt fabric.

For the filling use a Polyester.

Terylene comes in various grades:–

P2 used in cheaper quilts.

P3 a better filling for quilts. The manufacturer, I.C.I.,
claims that P3 retains its loft through continuous
washing.

Dacron Fiberfill is similar to P2 but manufactured
by Du Pont.

Making the tubes. Cut the fabric to the length and
width required.

Join the four strips together, making a double mitre
at each corner. Hand slip one edge to the edge of the
small quilt. Pad the border, and pin and handslip to the
quilt (Fig. 52).

Loose Covers

Loose-covers are an asset, especially on furniture that is subjected to constant use. They are expensive items, made from various fibres and mixtures of fibres. If the fabric used has not been pre-shrunk, the first laundering can be disastrous.

The cover may still fit reasonably widthways, but have shrunk lengthways. If the loose-cover has been tailored to a tie-under style; that is, the cover has been cut to extend under the base of the chair, originally giving a

FIG. 98.

very neat tailored appearance, it could now look like (Fig. 98). Instead of looking neat and tailored, the shrunken cover would be revealing the upholstery above the chair legs.

Making a skirt for this cover with a kick pleat at each corner is a satisfactory solution. (Fig. 99.)

FIG. 99.

Estimate for the fabric required; the depth of the skirt plus hem allowances, i.e. finished skirt length $7\frac{1}{2}$ inches (19 cm) plus one inch ($2\frac{1}{2}$ cm) for the lower hem, plus $\frac{1}{2}$ inch ($1\frac{1}{2}$ cm) at the top of the skirt where the skirt joins the loose-cover.

Measure the area around the chair and add 10 inches ($25\frac{1}{2}$ cm) at each corner for inverted pleats. (Fig. 100.) If the fabric purchased for the skirt is liable to shrink, launder before cutting. This type of skirt is best lined; use a cotton sateen curtain lining and launder before use. (Lining adds more weight so that the skirt hangs better. It also avoids a stitch line showing along the lower hem.)

Buy enough piping cord to pipe the lower edge of the

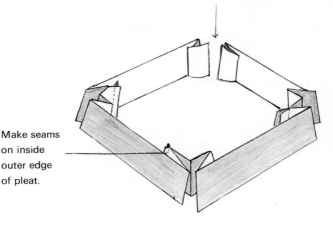

One corner left free
to accommodate opening
of loose-cover.

Make seams
on inside
outer edge
of pleat.

Fig. 100.

loose-cover plus shrinkage allowance; pre-shrink before use.

Place cover into position on the chair and, with tailors chalk, mark the approximate line of the joining of the skirt to the loose-cover.

Cut, leaving $\frac{1}{2}$ inch ($1\frac{1}{2}$ cm) sewing allowance on the loose-cover. Machine the lining to the skirt as Figs. 101 and 103 and pleat as (Fig. 100). Pipe the bottom edge of the loose-cover. Sew the skirt to the loose-cover. Press well.

Figs. 104 to 106. Show other forms of pleating used as skirts on loose-covers and bedcovers.

Even if shrinkage is not the problem, the cover may have become worn in the places that take extra strain, i.e. the tops of the arms where finger tips are often fidgeting and hands grasp when the sitter rises.

To renovate worn arms, cut away the worn piping and worn arm portions, and replace with fabric from the tuck-in. This is the part of the cover that tucks down out

141

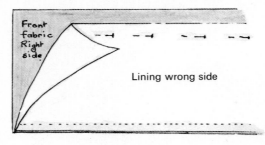

FIG. 101.

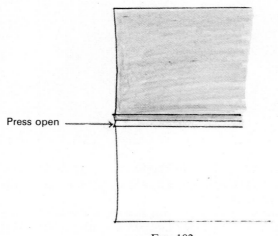

Press open

FIG. 102.

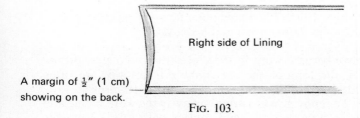

Right side of Lining

A margin of $\frac{1}{2}''$ (1 cm) showing on the back.

FIG. 103.

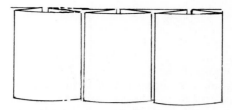

FIG. 104. Box pleats; estimate for 3 times the area they will occupy.

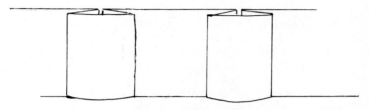

FIG. 105. Spaced box pleats; estimate for twice the area they will occupy.

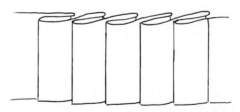

FIG. 106. Knife pleats; estimate for 3 times the area they will occupy.

of sight around the seat. Usually a good 6 inches (15 cm) has been allowed on this part of the chair. Be sure to replace the cut away parts with other fabric because, although out of sight, it is essential to the fit of the cover, as it helps to hold the cover in place while in use.

Should the worn parts require more cloth than that

available from the tuck-in, and the chair has a seat cushion, use part of the seat of the chair, replacing with other fabric.

If the chair does not have an accompanying seat cushion, unpick the outside back. Take a pattern of this before using it to repair the arms, and use the pattern to give a correct fit for the replacement.

Sometimes the only thing that distorts and shrinks on first cleaning or laundering is the piping. Then there is nothing for it but to unpick the piped seams and remake them, adding a little preshrunk cord where needed.

The openings on loose covers are usually secured with zip fasteners, but occasionally with a strap and fastening opening, on to which have been sewn hooks and eyes or press studs. After a first washing or cleaning there may be only a slight shrinkage, but enough to cause the openings to gape between the hooks and eyes or press studs. This is very unsightly and can be remedied by removing the present fasteners and replacing with a zip.

Bordered or box cushions. These are seat or back cushions made with loose-covers, and matching settee or chair covers. For worn piping, unpick and repipe with a contrast fabric. If the borders are also worn, use a contrast fabric for new borders and piping. Carefully unpick the cushions and use the old borders as a pattern. Remake as before.

Should the cushions be too worn to renovate, pick out a colour in the furniture covering, if it is patterned, and make new covers. If the material is plain and you cannot match it, then choose a contrasting colour.

Pillow cushions. Used for decoration, and as a comfortable support for the hollow of the back and as a head rest, these cushions can easily be remade in various ways.

A badly stained cushion should be completely unpicked. Cut the stained part away, and with other remnants of fabric make a cushion with contrast panels.

Alternatively, use part of the present cover with another fabric and make a patchwork cushion. Or appliqué

144

another fabric in a pleasing shape over a stained or worn area.

If only the piping is worn, unpick the cushion, trim that and any other worn parts away, and remake.

Brighten cushions that you are tired of by decorating with fringe or braid. Plain cushions can be embroidered by machine or hand.

Making new inner case for a down and feather or down seat, or a back bordered cushion. This type of inner case has horizontal walls which keep the feather filling evenly

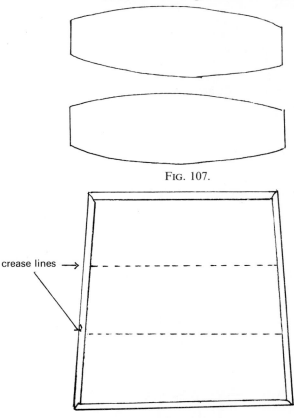

FIG. 107.

crease lines →

FIG. 108.

K

distributed. The walls are deeper at the centre by approximately 1 inch (2 cm), tapering off to the depth of the border at the ends. The inner case should be made of a good downproof fabric.

Make a paper pattern of the required size of the cushion. Cut the top and bottom of the cushion plus $\frac{1}{2}$ inch (1 cm) seam allowance on each side. Cut the borders so as to have a seam on each corner. Allow $\frac{1}{2}$ inch (1 cm) on all edges. Cut the two walls to extend across the width of the cushion, again allowing $\frac{1}{2}$ inch (1 cm) seam allowance on the edges. (Fig. 107.)

Press a $\frac{1}{2}$ inch (1 cm) single fold on the four sides of the cushion, top and bottom. (Fig. 108.)

Make and press two folds across the width of the top and bottom pieces. These are the lines to follow when machining the walls into position. (Fig. 100.) Sew the walls to the lines indicated, making sure that the ends of

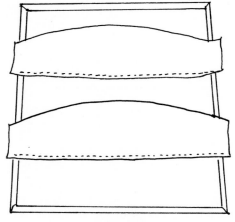

Fig. 109.

the walls extend for $\frac{1}{2}$ inch (1 cm) beyond the sides of the cushion. (Fig. 109). This is essential, as this is the portion that is sewn to the side borders. (Fig. 111.) Seam together the four pieces of the border. Press the edges over with a single $\frac{1}{2}$ inch (1 cm) fold. (Fig. 110.)

146

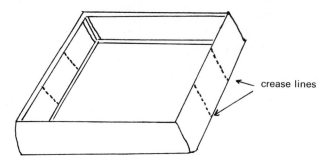

crease lines

FIG. 110.

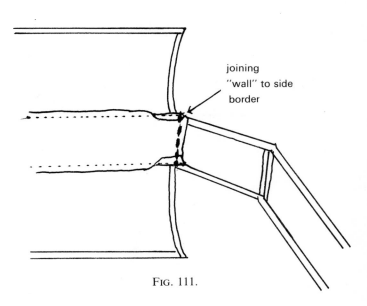

joining
"wall" to side
border

FIG. 111.

Make two crease marks on the side border in line with the machining that is holding the walls on the top and bottom of the cushion. (Fig. 110.) Sew the ends of the walls to the crease lines on the side borders. (Fig. 111.) Sew the cushion top and bottom by 'top stitching',

147

which means sewing together edge to edge on the right side of the cushion.

Leave an opening into each section for the application of the filling. (Fig. 112.)

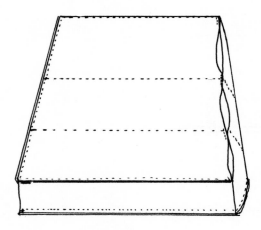

Fig. 112.

CHAPTER EIGHTEEN

Care of Soft Furnishings

Keep curtain tracks dust free, occasionally give metal tracks a rub with a little silicone furniture cream.

Clean discoloured or rusted hooks and rings, either by boiling in vinegar for a few minutes or soaking in cloudy ammonia, and rub dry. For plastic tracks, simply clean with a damp soapy cloth and wipe dry. Nylon fittings, hooks and rings, wash in soapy water, rinse and wipe dry.

Some soft furnishings, because of the very nature of the sewing construction, would be difficult to home launder, and sometimes the fibres and weave of the cloth make it more suitable for dry-cleaning. It is often difficult, with the wide range of fibres and new techniques around, to identify the fibre content by its appearance and feel. The adaptability of man-made fibres enables them to be made into a large number of different fabrics that may resemble fabric made from natural fibres. The wide use of different fibre mixtures and blends also make this form of identification difficult. For this reason, save any labels given at the time the fabric is purchased.

Many reputable furnishing departments pass on the necessary information by supplying labels giving washing or dry-cleaning instructions. These are known as 'Care Labels'.

Care Labelling – H.L.C.C. Scheme. Care Labelling, telling you have to wash and how to set your iron for different fabrics, helps to achieve the best results. The Home Laundering Consultative Council (representing

	Instructions		Examples of application

<table>
<tr><th colspan="2">MACHINE</th><th>HAND WASH</th></tr>
<tr><td>Very hot maximum wash (85°C) to boil</td><td></td><td>Hand-hot (48°C) or boil</td></tr>
<tr><td colspan="3">Spin or wring</td></tr>
</table>

White cotton and linen, without special finishes.

<table>
<tr><th colspan="2">MACHINE</th><th>HAND WASH</th></tr>
<tr><td>Hot maximum wash (60°C)</td><td></td><td>Hand-hot (48°C)</td></tr>
<tr><td colspan="3">Spin or wring</td></tr>
</table>

Cotton, linen and rayon without special finishes where colour fastness is satisfactory at 60°C (140°F).

<table>
<tr><th colspan="2">MACHINE</th><th>HAND WASH</th></tr>
<tr><td>Hot medium wash (60°C)</td><td></td><td>Hand-hot (48°C)</td></tr>
<tr><td colspan="3">Cold rinse. Short spin or drip-dry</td></tr>
</table>

White polyamide (nylon).

<table>
<tr><th colspan="2">MACHINE</th><th>HAND WASH</th></tr>
<tr><td>Hand-hot medium wash (48°C)</td><td></td><td>Hand-hot (48°C)</td></tr>
<tr><td colspan="3">Cold rinse. Short spin or drip-dry</td></tr>
</table>

Coloured polyamide (nylon), polyester cotton and rayon with special finishes and acrylic cotton mixtures.

<table>
<tr><th colspan="2">MACHINE</th><th>HAND WASH</th></tr>
<tr><td>Warm medium wash (40°C)</td><td></td><td>Warm (40°C)</td></tr>
<tr><td colspan="3">Spin or wring</td></tr>
</table>

Cotton, linen and rayon where colour fastness is satisfactory at 40°C (104°F) but not at 60°C (140°F).

<table>
<tr><th colspan="2">MACHINE</th><th>HAND WASH</th></tr>
<tr><td>Warm minimum wash (40°C)</td><td></td><td>Warm (40°C)</td></tr>
<tr><td colspan="3">Cold rinse. Short spin. Do not wring</td></tr>
</table>

Acetate, acrylic, triacetate and mixtures of these fibres with wool and polyester/wool mixtures.

Wool and wool mixtures.

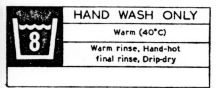

Washable pleated articles containing acrylic, polyamide (nylon) polyester and triacetate.

FIG. 113. Washing instructions devised by the Home Laundering Consultative Council.

the textile industry, the domestic appliance industry, washing product manufacturers, distributors and allied interests) have established a labelling scheme as illustrated. (Fig. 113.) The eight numbered processes appear in full on soap and detergent packs and in washing machine instructions, and are used individually on textile care labels together with ironing, dry cleaning and/or cautionary advice where required. The iron settings recommended by the H.L.C.C. are set out below and are becoming standardised on all irons produced in this country.

H.L.C.C. Iron Settings

Setting	Description	Corresponding to a safe ironing test temperature	Type of fibre

151

No. 1	Cool	100°C	acrylics (Acrilan Courtelle, Orlon)
No. 2	Warm	150°C	Acetate, nylon, Terylene, Tricel, Wool.
No. 3	Medium Hot	180°C	Rayon
No. 4	Hot	200°C	Cotton, linen

Dry clean the following: velvets, velours, chenilles, tapestries, brocades and fabrics containing silk or wool. **Wash,** colour-fast cottons and linens, both plain and printed, and linen mixtures; Terylene, knitted nylon, flat Dralon (not Dralon velvet) and glass fibre

Net Curtains. Net curtains, or glass curtains as they are sometimes called, because they hang immediately next to the glass and behind the heavier draw curtains, protect the draw curtains from the dirt and smoke of the atmosphere, the net acting as a filter to the air flowing through the window.

Nets made from man-made fibres, such as Terylene, have low moisture absorption. This means they are easy to wash. Launder frequently. If heavily soiled, soak beforehand for at least 15 minutes in soapy water or detergent. After this the stains will loosen. Wash the curtains in the recommended manner. Use a medium wash. Avoid rubbing or twisting, just gently squeeze, or else machine wash for a minimum period. Rinse well in cold water, lightly spin, do not wring and hang to dry. Drying will not take long. Iron with a cool iron while still slightly damp. Terylene net can be drip dried and hung back in place.

Glass fibre. Glass fibre curtains should be washed by hand only.

Remove hooks or rings. Avoid rubbing or excessive

squeezing. Wash in warm water using soap or detergent. Rinse in clear warm water.

Allow the curtains to drip dry, or gently roll in a towel to remove excess moisture, and, with care, rehang while damp.

Do not iron.

Do not dry clean or machine wash.

Velour curtains. Lightly brush frequently with a soft brush in the direction of the pile. Dry clean only.

No matter how carefully velour curtains are packed, crushing in transit is a problem. Crushing alters the angle of the pile, and in consequence the reflection of the light. This shows up in the form of patches of dark and light shading. Freshly hung velour curtains do not do justice to this beautiful pile fabric, but as the atmosphere lifts the pile, the appearance will steadily improve. This improvement can continue for several months.

To improve very bad patches of creasing, hang in a steamy bathroom. Rehang, gently smoothing with a soft brush or cloth.

Lining greatly improves the 'hang' and general appearance of the curtains, and is really essential.

A corded curtain track is recommended, as grasping, particularly with long finger-nails, can cause crushing and actual damage.

Chintz curtains. A cotton fabric that can be home laundered; most chintzs have a semi-permanent finish. This glaze will gradually weaken as washing proceeds. Starching after the final rinse will help to restore the original finish.

Iron while the fabric is still damp, with a hot iron, using plenty of pressure, till the fabric is absolutely dry. Washing code, 5, ironing 4.

Loose-covers. Traditional loose-covers made of cretonne, linen, linen union, repp or damask are expensive items; being individually tailored and requiring a skilled upholstress to make them. An asset on furniture that is subjected to constant use, they can be washed or dry cleaned according to fibre content.

Remove, shake and brush well. Repair if necessary.

153

Test for colour fastness before washing. Dry clean or wash by hand or machine. Rinse well, spin and hang to dry.

Iron while still damp; press on the wrong side. Press seams and frills or pleats well.

Fit back on to the furniture and smooth into position while still slightly damp.

Stretch Nylon loose-covers. Stretch nylon loose-covers are easy to wash, quick to dry and need no ironing. High strength and excellent dimensional stability makes nylon safe to wash repeatedly.

Nylon fabrics should be washed frequently, using hand hot water, by machine or by hand. Do not boil as this would set creases permanently. Use a good soap or detergent, plenty of water, and rinse throughly. Give a final cold rinse, short spin or drip dry.

Removable cushion covers belonging to furniture upholstered in Dralon velvet must not be washed because of the cotton ground; dry clean only. To remove creases from Dralon velvet iron on the wrong side using a damp cloth and with the iron set at nylon. The cloth should be ironed in the direction of the pile. Avoid making the cloth too wet and do not allow the iron to rest on any one part of the cloth.

Bedspreads and quilts. Candlewick bedcovers should be washed rather than cleaned. Treat as a blanket and rinse thoroughly.

Candlewick bedcovers require frequent shaking during the drying period to fluff up the tufted pile. Do not iron.

Crocheted bedcovers should be gently stretched back to shape while still damp. If the bedcover is made from silk, rayon or wool tapestry, or trimmed with braids, or made of two fabrics of different fibres, dry clean.

Quilts. Man-made wadded quilts can be laundered at home providing adequate space is available to wash and rinse thoroughly. If not, send them to a laundry who will be more capable of dealing with them.

Small man-made quilts of cot size could be managed more satisfactorarily at home than the larger sizes.

The traditional eiderdown is best cleaned by professional dry cleaners. Laundering at home tends to make the feathers and down matt together. The coin operated dry-cleaning unit could be used, but always remember to air the cleaned article out of doors after dry cleaning, as fumes still present in the fabric from the cleaning agent used can be lethal in a confined airless space.

Pelmets. Pelmets mounted on upholsterers buckram must be dry cleaned only. Take down from the window and brush well. Roll up and take to the cleaners. After three or four cleanings the buckram will become soft and brittle, and it will then be time for renewal, or a remake with a new foundation of buckram.

Spot cleaning. For spot removal of small stains keep a proprietary brand of dry cleaner handy. These come in bottles and aerosol cans. Do not attempt to use these over large areas.

Trichlorethylene (which is sold under various trade names) is particularly satisfactory as it has general solvent properties and is completely non-inflammable. But always read the information on the containers very carefully before use and follow the instructions given, especially the safety precautions. Some solvents are inflammable. The stains removed by solvents are mostly grease, oil or materials with a greasy base such as butter, tar, shoe-polish and make-up.

The greasy marks can be removed from wool, cotton, linen, nylon, terylene, felt and silk, but do not use solvents on P.V.C., rubberised or foam backed materials, furs, leather or suede.

On non-washable fabrics, test for colour fastness; on a loose-cover use an inner hem or the tuck-in, on a curtain unpick a small portion of the lower hem; damp, place a white cloth on top and press hard. If the dye is not fast the solvent will dissolve it and transfer it to the white cloth beneath. If this happens do not continue but have the article dry-cleaned professionally.

Where the dye proves to be fast, place a white cloth beneath the stain. This is important to prevent the stain being transferred to another part of the article.

With another clean cloth soaked in solvent, rub in a circle, starting outside the stain and work in towards the centre. This avoids the common fault of pushing the stain outwards so that it leaves a ring.

Finally air the article thoroughly.

For the accidental spillage of tea, coffee or alcohol on loose-covers that are washable, successful stain removal depends on quick action. Rinse the stained cover in cold water. Cold water is important, as hot water can set stains. Leave soaking in cold water till the loose cover can be washed in the normal way.

For non-washable removable covers, blot up the spillage immediately and take the cover to the local dry cleaners as soon as possible, telling him the nature of the stain and fibre content of the fabric if possible. Do not use trial and error methods yourself, risking damage to the fabric.

Remember that the day-to-day care of soft furnishings is just as important as major renovation work and may, in fact, avoid the need for such renovation.

Index

157

Index